ABRAHADABRA

ABRAHADABRA

Understanding Aleister Crowley's Thelemic Magick

Rodney Orpheus

WEISERBOOKS
San Francisco, CA / Newburyport, MA

This edition first published in 2005 by
RED WHEEL/WEISER, LLC

With offices at:
665 Third Street, Suite 400
San Francisco, CA 94107
www.redwheelweiser.com

First published in 1995 by
Looking Glass Press, Stockholm, Sweden.

Library of Congress Cataloging-in-Publication Data

Orpheus, Rodney.
  Abrahadabra : understanding Aleister Crowley's thelemic magick /
Rodney Orpheus.
    p. cm.
  Includes bibliographical references.
  ISBN 1-57863-326-5
  1. Magic. 2. Occultism. 3. Crowley, Aleister, 1875-1947. I. Title.
  BF1611.O77 2005
  133.4'3--dc22   2005008217

Text design by STUDIO 31
www.studio31.com

Typeset in Adobe Sabon

Printed in the United States of America

8   7   6   5   4   3   2

CONTENTS

INTRODUCTION
TO THE 2005 EDITION

Do what thou wilt shall be the whole of the Law.

This is the second version of this foreword that I've written for this new edition of *Abrahadabra*. After reading my first attempt, the author (speaking with the voice of candor reserved exclusively for the best of friends and the bitterest of enemies) lamented that it was a "potted bio" of Aleister Crowley that missed the mark entirely. While I remain firm in my belief that it was a damned good "potted bio," I must confess I see the wisdom of his criticisms.

Abrahadabra is not about Aleister Crowley and should not be colored by his history, reputation, or personality. *Abrahadabra* is about the practice of the magick of Thelema—a system of physical, mental, and spiritual training and discipline based on two fundamental principles: "Do what thou wilt shall be the whole of the Law" and "Love is the law, love under will."

By writing this book, the author reveals his profound understanding of the "Do" in "Do what thou wilt ... " and challenges and inspires the reader to share his commitment to action rather than argument, deeds rather than platitudes, experience rather than theories.

He succeeds mightily at this. He fails, however, at keeping his own personality out of the text—and for this the reader should be deeply grateful. His casual and humorous style serves to lower the blood pressure and causes one to immediately identify on a personal level with his thoughts, attitudes, and conclusions.

It takes a particular (some say peculiar) kind of individual to write unpretentiously and unhypocritically about the practical aspects of Thelemic Magick. Rodney Orpheus, unlike many practicing (and published) occultists, has a life. He is a rock star, a recording artist, a business executive, and a high-degree initiate officer of one of the most revered and influential magical societies in the world. His life, however, does not revolve around any of these. In true Thelemic style, they each revolve around *him*. So it should be for all who tread the way of Thelema, a path where the individual and the individual's true Will is the focus of the Great Work.

But where does one start the "work" of the Great Work? Without some kind of beginner's guide, studying and practicing Thelemic Magick is like trying to learn to swim by jumping into the deep end of the pool and doing whatever you have to do to keep from drowning. Many have done just that and (having survived the ordeal and human nature being what it is) carry the machismo attitude of, "I did it the hard way, so should everybody else." This attitude is, to quote Al Franken's new age counselor, Stuart Smalley, just *stinkin' thinkin'*.

There will always be ordeals—with or without helpful manuals such as this—and no one can presume to judge the circumstances of another's magical life. Mr. Orpheus had the benefit of life in Holy Orders and the mentorship of initiate instructors. Even with these enviable advantages, I'm sure he will be the first to admit that his early studies and practices were plagued unnecessarily with time-consuming confusion as to how best to proceed.

Abrahadabra is a precious gift to all who wish to immediately embark upon the fundamental practices and meditations of Thelemic Magick and assure themselves that their magical careers are being built on a firm and balanced foundation. I am delighted to see it appear in this new edition.

Love is the law, love under will.

LON MILO DUQUETTE
COSTA MESA, CALIFORNIA

INTRODUCTION

Do what thou wilt shall be the whole of the Law

Thelemic Magick? Why Thelemic? Isn't magick just magick? And what is so special about this Thelemic stuff anyway? All I want is a good, comprehensive beginner's book on magick. Why does it seem so difficult for you magicians to write one?

All good questions that I've been asked many times in the past few years, and in response to which I have written this book. I have tried to make it as clear and comprehensive a guide to Thelema as possible. All the way through its writing I have checked it and re-checked it, tested every exercise carefully, and used the text to teach others; all to ensure that it would be a book that really was simple and straightforward. Just to write this small book took me four years of effort, not to mention the decade of personal magical work that came before it. I don't claim that this is the perfect beginner's book, but it's probably as close as you'll get at this time.

Thelemic magick is largely the legacy of one man, Aleister Crowley (rhymes with holy—many people pronounce it wrong). You have probably already heard of Crowley—most people think that they know something about him. My first recommendation is that you forget all the stories you've heard—at least 50 percent of them are total rubbish. You don't have to like Crowley to perform Thelemic magick—I know several Thelemites who do not particularly like his personality—but he is without doubt the single most important figure in modern magical history. This book is based largely on his work, and I will be quoting his writings frequently in the chapters to follow.

So what is Thelemic magick? Crowley defined magick as: "The Science and Art of causing Change in accordance with the Will." Like any science, magick has different schools and branches, and like any art, it has different styles. This book concentrates solely on one branch of magick—Thelemic magick. This is not as much of a limitation as it may at first appear. The Thelemic system is a synthesis of much that was best from earlier forms of occult learning, plus totally new parts specifically designed for the modern world we inhabit. It forms a complete guide to magick for the New Aeon dawning across our planet.

It is very difficult for most magicians to write simply about magick, because, well, it's not a simple subject. Every part of it links with everything else, so to a newcomer it can often seem like a tangled ball of thread, each bit wrapped so tightly around the other bits that it's impossible to even know where to start. So for the convenience of the reader I have divided it into three main aspects: meditation, ritual, and philosophy. The eleven chapters of this book deal with part of each aspect in turn. Chapters 1, 4, 7, and 10 deal with meditation, chapters 2, 5, 8, and 11 with ritual, and chapters 3, 6, and 9 with philosophy. Although I have split up the book into these three aspects, it should be remembered that magick contains all of them in equal proportion, and each aspect is connected with each other aspect. In order to learn one, you must learn the others too. By dealing with part of each subject in turn, you will hopefully learn in a balanced, gradual manner. The beginning meditation exercises in chapter 1 will assist you to understand chapter 2, the ritual in chapter 2 will help you to understand the philosophy expounded in chapter 3, and all these three combined help you to move on to the more complicated meditation exercises which appear in chapter 4, and so on.

The other advantage in dealing with the subject in phases like this is that it enables the student to "get up and go" right away. You do not have to read the entire book in order to start working. In fact, if you are a total beginner to Thelemic magick, I recommend that you do *not* read the entire book in one go. The best bet is to read each chapter one at a time, and when you have read through the entire chapter, go back and attempt to work through the exercises given. You should endeavor to do each exercise as it is described, in the order in which it is described. Many of the exercises are given in a short form, with explanatory notes immediately afterward. Make sure to read the notes thoroughly before you start the exercise. After every third chapter, take a break and spend some time reviewing what you have learned in the previous three.

Thelema is about *personal* development, and this means *you* have to do the work for yourself. Simply reading this book is not enough. It doesn't matter how great your theoretical knowledge is, unless you live it you are wasting your time. Knowledge is not the same thing as understanding, please remember this.

It is likely that you will feel more attracted to one of the aspects than to the others, and this is normal, but you should remember while working through the book that all three strands should be studied with equal care and intensity if you want to develop your talents fully. Unbalanced development may seem easier and faster at first, but in the long term it can become extremely limiting.

Some readers may also find the philosophical concepts a little difficult at the beginning, so I have tried to make this aspect easier to cope with by giving meditation exercises that allow abstract concepts to be grasped directly through the reader's own experiences.

If you bought this book expecting glamorous rituals featuring multitudes of evil demons and the deflowering of naked virgins, I'm afraid you may be a little disappointed—at least at first. Evocation of demons and naked priestesses on the altar do have their part to play in Thelemic magick, don't worry (hey, that's half the fun!), but I advise you not to attempt to fly before you can walk. Magical rituals, because of the huge power they contain, can cause great stress on the body and mind of an unprepared magician, so it is best if you spend plenty of time on the basic preparatory exercises in the first few chapters before tackling the more hardcore stuff in the second half of the book. I know that practicing the same simple stuff day after day for months on end can get pretty boring (it bored the hell out of me), but it's worth it in the end, for your magical powers will be massively increased and your capacity for both working and playing will become much, much greater.

Although this book is by no means large, I have tried to make it as comprehensive as possible, and it contains enough exercises to keep even the most talented magician busy for at least a year; but I don't pretend to be the fount of all wisdom. Those of you who wish to study Thelemic magick more closely would be well advised to consult other texts as well, particularly those by Aleister Crowley. I strongly advise the reader to get hold of a copy of Crowley's *Magick*, which is really a compendium of three books, *Book 4* parts 1 and 2 and *Magick in Theory and Practice*, plus many other shorter books in its appendices. *Magick* is a book that contains enough magical knowledge to keep you studying it for many years. *Magick without Tears*, a collection of Crowley's letters to his pupils, is also useful for the beginner. The most important Thelemic text of all, however, is *Liber AL vel Legis—The Book of the Law*. This is, ultimately, the source of all Thelemic magick, but is very, very difficult for the beginner to understand. For this reason I highly recommend that all readers get hold of a copy of *The Law Is for All*, which contains the complete text of Liber AL plus detailed commentaries on each of the verses. At the end of each chapter of this book, I will list some references to these books so that students can follow up ideas in more detail if desired. The compendium of works entitled *Gems from the Equinox* is also valuable, either in addition to, or instead of, the preceding volumes, as it contains most of the important appendices from *Magick*, as well as *Liber AL* and many other useful texts.

I also highly recommend that you invest in a pack of tarot cards, for these will come in very handy indeed during the work you are about to do. There are many tarot packs in existence, 90 percent of them being completely worthless. The best one for our purposes is the pack designed by Aleister Crowley and drawn by Lady Frieda Harris, usually called the Crowley-Thoth Tarot. If you can't get hold of this tarot (and it should not be difficult, it's the single most popular pack in the world), another excellent pack for beginners is the Tarot of Ceremonial Magick by Lon and Constance DuQuette, which I highly recommend.

I am aware that one of the biggest problems facing many people who approach magick for the first time is the "magical jargon" used. Students are always asking me why I will use a Latin or Sanskrit word instead of using plain English. This is a very important point, and I have tried where possible to keep jargon to a minimum. However, like any science, magick has terms and concepts that are difficult to describe in ordinary language, since we are dealing with extraordinary things. Wherever I have used magical jargon, I have tried to explain it as carefully as possible, but I do advise you that as you read the book you take the time to read over any terms that are unfamiliar to you and try to make sure that you understand what I'm getting at before you move on.

I have one other important recommendation for the student setting out along the Royal Road to Wisdom—keep a record! This is absolutely vital. You should obtain a good-sized notebook and write in this Magical Diary every day. Like a good scientist, note down all conditions prevailing during every magical experiment: time, weather, your thoughts, emotions, and desires, everything large and small. Remember that you are performing important experiments, and keeping records of all experiments is vital; but unlike the conventional scientist, you are performing experiments on yourself, not on some inert substance, so your feelings at the end of each working are the most important part to be recorded. Your Magical Diary will help you to order your thoughts (and believe me your thoughts will become very disordered as you work through this book!) and also build up to form a reference work that you can consult to see just how far you have progressed. When you read back through your Diary after a few month's work, you will be able to see the habitual patterns of expression and feeling that you tend to fall into, you will see where you may have made a mistake and not noticed it at the time, etc. You will be able to analyze yourself and your actions and reactions much more closely. Above the portal of initiation are inscribed the words "Know Thyself"; this self-knowledge is your goal, and the Magical Diary the primary tool to help you achieve it.

Remember always: magick is a subtle and curious thing, and often works in ways you do not expect, and at times you do not expect—but it *always* works. Every magical act brings a result, as you are about to learn ...

CHAPTER ONE

BASIC YOGA: ASANA

Yoga? What's that got to do with magick? Isn't it some sort of health exercise?

Well, yes, it is some sort of health exercise. It is also the foundation stone of all practical Thelemic magick. It is important to remember that learning magick is not just a case of learning how to wave a wand around while chanting strange spells—although don't worry, you'll be doing plenty of that later. To fully learn magick, you must learn everything about yourself, because it is from you yourself that the magick will spring. So knowing your own being is the first duty and desire of all good magicians.

OK. I know what you're thinking: how can tying myself up in knots help me know myself? It is important at first to rid yourself of a common misconception: that yoga means standing on your head cross-legged chanting long complicated sentences. You can do that if you want, but it may not help you much, especially when you fall down and break your neck.

The first and most important thing to learn in yoga is posture, or asana to use the correct term. Since many yoga terms do not translate exactly into English I will sometimes use the original Sanskrit word. Don't worry if this is confusing at the start, it is quite easy to get used to.

But back to asana. It is important for you to learn a good posture for several reasons. First, asana is useful while meditating. It helps keep your body still and cuts down the amount of fidgeting your body gets up to if it is left to its own devices. Try this simple exercise. Take a look at your watch and note what time it is. Now put this book down, and simply sit still for a few minutes, staring at only one thing all the while—the cover of the book for example. When you begin to get really uncomfortable or itchy, stop and check the time on your watch. If you managed more than a few minutes without discomfort, you're doing pretty good.

So now let's think about this exercise. You can't sit still and concentrate for more than a few minutes. How are you going to do a ritual which might take an hour of total mental and physical effort?

The second reason why asana is important is that particular postures affect the subtle areas of your body in different ways, strengthening parts of your being which are going to come under stress when you start exploring the astral plane later in your studies.

The third main reason why an asana is useful, and why it is different than just simply "sitting still," is that your posture affects the flow of energy to the magical centers in your body. These magical centers are called chakras, or "wheels." There are seven main chakras, which are as follows.

At the base of the spine is the Muladhara chakra, the "Earth center" of your body. At your genital region is the Svadisthana chakra or "Moon center." Around your stomach is the Manipura, associated with the energies of Venus and Mercury, and above that is the heart center, Anahata, the seat of the Sun's energies. In your throat is the Vishuddha chakra, attributed to Pluto, the center of transformation; in your forehead is the Ajna chakra, where the energies of Saturn and Uranus are gathered, and right above your head is the Sahasrara, the ultimate chakric center, attributed to the planet Neptune. Don't worry if you can't remember all these Sanskrit names or if you can't understand what the planets have to do with it, this will slowly begin to make sense with practice. The main thing to remember now is that these centers exist and act as reservoirs of magical energy which you can draw upon when you are in need. If you like, study the diagram of the chakric system and try to imagine these centers inside your body whirling with energy as you sit in your asana.

So what exactly is an asana? The great yoga teacher Patanjali wrote that "Asana is that which is firm and pleas-

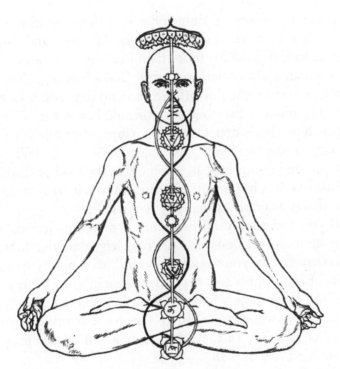

THE SEVEN CHAKRAS

ant." It's that simple. The most basic asana is known as the God posture. It consists of sitting on a straight-backed, fairly firm chair, legs close together, with your hands resting on your knees. If you have ever seen statues of Egyptian gods sitting, you'll know what I mean.

"You mean that's it?" I hear you cry.

Well, it's a start anyway.

"So why haven't I seen Indian yogis sitting like this?"

Good question. Indian holy men don't tend to live in apartments, and they don't usually have enough room in their loincloths to fit a chair in. Normally they sit on the ground, because the ground is cheap, and it's always there.

The last paragraph was a bit of exaggeration actually, but still contains an element of truth. There are some advantages to postures where you sit on the ground, so try them out to see which you prefer. Remember that the most important thing is that the posture should feel good for you and should continue to feel good for more than just a few minutes.

You can try a variation on the God posture, called the Dragon. Kneel on the floor (I recommend that you fold up a blanket to make a firm but comfortable base), toes of both feet touching, heels apart, forming a sort of saddle for your buttocks to rest on. Keep your legs together and place your hands on top of your legs, like you did in the God posture. As in all asanas, it is important to keep your back fairly straight. Again this is a simple asana, but very useful.

If you feel totally athletic and/or masochistic, you can try the famous Lotus posture; sit cross-legged on the floor (or blanket) and place your hands on your knees, palms upward, the tip of the thumb and first finger touching to form an O shape, the other fingers fairly straight but relaxed. This is my personal favorite asana, but if you have trouble with it, remember that any of the other asanas will do the jobs we have in mind just as well.

OK. You've picked your asana, now what do you do with it? For now, not a lot. The first exercise we're going to do is very easy. Sit in your asana, close your eyes, and simply concentrate on your breathing. Feel your breath flowing through your nostrils, down your neck, filling your lungs. Don't attempt to control your breathing at all, just let it flow naturally. As you breathe in, mentally say the words,

The breath flows in.

And as you breathe out, think,

The breath flows out.

Note that you are *not* saying that it is *you* that is breathing. This is important. We want to let the breath flow totally outside your conscious control—in this exercise you are only an observer of the process. You are establishing the "Silent Watcher"; learning to detach yourself from your basic bodily responses. This is not meant to imply that your bodily responses are "evil" or "dirty," or that the body is something that you must attempt to escape from—far from it. Your soul has chosen to incarnate in your body for a purpose, but until you can become aware of the extent of your body's abilities, you will never fully understand that purpose. By becoming the Silent Watcher, you will learn to appreciate more fully the processes of sensation, of how your being is linked on many levels—breath, thought, emotion, Will, etc. Do this exercise at least once every day for the first month of your magical training—I guarantee that after a month of just this alone you will feel quite different inside. Don't forget to keep a careful record of your feelings in your Magical Diary.

As you begin to practice asana, you will probably find yourself hitting a point (usually after about ten minutes or so) where you begin to feel extremely uncomfortable; your muscles may become cramped, and the overall feeling may be one of agony. Try not to give up at this point, but note when it happens in your Magical Diary and attempt to work at the asana just a *little* bit longer, even though it hurts. Be careful not to go too far—you don't want to end up damaging yourself. In general, remember that keeping your yoga practice regular is more important than making it long-lasting. Ten minutes every day is much better than just an hour on Sunday.

It is best to try to do your yoga practice at about the same time every day, to get into a rhythm. Since yoga is also much easier when you do not have too much food in your stomach, by far the best time is in the morning, just after you get up. Failing that, just before you go to bed at night is also good. You should definitely not practice just after you have eaten, as too much of your body's energy is involved with digesting your food, and you will feel sluggish and sleepy. You are probably thinking that you also feel sluggish and sleepy first thing in the morning as well—but this is different. Performing your yoga immediately after waking will help your body wake itself up, by circulating the chemicals that you need much faster than normal. Do *not* drink tea or coffee immediately on waking—over a long period of time artificial stimulants actually slow down the production of the body's own stimulants. If you are a caffeine addict, wait until after your yoga practice for your first fix. After six months you'll feel a lot better for it.

Obviously you will feel rather uncomfortable practicing your asana while wearing your normal clothes, so try to wear something loose and reasonably warm; jogging clothes are OK, but not perfect. I find that it is much easier (especially in the Lotus position), if I am not wearing anything on my legs at all. If your room is warm enough, try working naked—I don't recommend you wear rings or bracelets, though a necklace is fine, preferably one which has a magical meaning to you. Probably the best thing you can wear is a long loose robe. This should be made of silk or cotton and ideally be plain black in color, though white, gold, or deep blue would do in a pinch. Avoid having a robe with a design or pattern on it—the simpler the better. A Japanese style silk kimono is quite nice and easy to get hold of. The absolute best is a robe which has no opening at the front, but which goes over the head and down to your ankles. It should be wide enough at the bottom to allow unimpeded movement and to allow you to sit with your legs folded up comfortably inside it. The sleeves should similarly widen toward the ends so that you can also fold your arms inside them. If possible, a large hood which can cover your whole head is also a very good idea. When you are performing your meditation exercise the hood can act to cut out a lot of the ambient light and noise (and it looks cool if you're covered in black from head to toe—black is so very flattering to the figure). Do not use your robe for anything other than magical purposes and keep it away from everyday things that might soil it—like cooking with hot oil or cleaning the bathroom (don't laugh, I've seen it done).

You may well find that during your asana you become hypersensitive to outside influences, which is ironic, because that is the very thing that we are attempting to overcome. Street sounds especially can be a real problem; in addition, you will be able to hear everything that is going on outside your house. There is no ready solution to this, basically you just have to work through it. After a while you will find yourself becoming able to screen out the noises that you do not wish to hear; you will still hear the noises, but as your body learns to enter stillness more fully, noises simply become irrelevant, they no longer disturb you in any way.

If you find that the noise is really so excessive that you cannot even begin to concentrate, you can always play some music while you work. This should be as minimal as possible, either long slow meandering New Age type synthesizer music or ethnic music with a religious basis, such as traditional Indian music for example. Music is not really a good solution, however. One other interesting technique is to use white noise. White noise is sound which contains all frequencies at once, in the same way that white light contains all light frequencies. The easiest way to obtain white noise is to tune a television or radio to one end of its tuning range, where there is no broadcast signal. You will hear a loud hissing noise. Some people find white noise very useful, some people are driven to distraction by it; so just try it and see.

Another common problem during asana is the tongue problem. You know where to put your hands and where to put your feet, but many people find that as they lose awareness of the rest of their body, their tongue seems to become huge and possessed of a life of its own. My tip is to roll the tongue back in the mouth, so that the tip of your tongue is pressing against the roof of your mouth, near the soft part at the back. This may seem a little uncomfortable at first, but it has yogic properties that make it very useful for meditation.

The most dangerous problem of all is success. "What?" cries the reader, "How can success be a problem?" It is a problem in that after some practice you may well find yourself achieving wondrous mystical states, flying into white light, discovering the body of God, etc. Although these states can be very pleasant (and cheaper than psychedelic drugs), you must be very wary of thinking that you have found the answer to all your searching. Believe me, this is *nothing* compared to what you are going to get later. Enjoy these exalted states for a little while, but remember that they are not the results we are looking for. Ultimately these things are distractions, will-o'-the-wisps that should not be followed into the marsh that will ensnare you. Stay on the path of the humble pilgrim!

FURTHER STUDY

Magick—Part I, Chapter 1
Magick—Appendix VII: Liber E vel Exercitiorum, Part III

CHAPTER TWO

YOUR FIRST RITUAL: THE PENTAGRAM

Ritual is the outward expression of magical work. But what exactly is a ritual, and why do we do it?

A ritual is a sequence of acts, gestures, and words which we perform in order to achieve a specific result. Take for example starting a car. When you first learned to drive (assuming you have learned), you had to go through a long rigmarole—check the hand brake, check that the car is not in gear, put the key in the ignition, turn it, check the choke, rev the engine, etc. Even when you have been driving for years, you still must do all these things in a particular way, in a particular order. Of course, after you have done these things a thousand times, they are easy and natural—but they are not at all natural when you first start learning. So it is with ritual. Ritual frequently seems unnatural, difficult to remember, and sometimes just plain silly. The important thing is that it works, and that is something that you must never forget. But it also has to be done carefully and in the right sequence.

The most well-known, basic ritual is referred to as the Lesser Banishing Ritual of the Pentagram, or more simply as the pentagram ritual (sometimes abbreviated to the letters LBRP). This is not really one specific ritual, but rather a framework that can be developed into a personalized daily ritual. It is called a Banishing Ritual, which means that it has as its primary purpose the banishing or cleansing of the magician's working environment, getting rid of all unwanted forces, i.e., of all forces except the ones you need. The nature of banishing is frequently misunderstood—I have seen several occult textbooks which state that a banishing ritual gets rid of all negative influences. This is *not* true! A good banishing will get rid of *all* forces, both positive *and* negative, leaving a completely neutral atmosphere for the magician to work in. After all, when you wash your clothes, you don't just wash away some dirt and leave the rest, do you?

It is always important to remember that positive and negative do not mean the same thing as good and bad. Positive and negative are only two polarities of the same force, and both are necessary for the force to work. Think of a battery—it has positive and negative ends, but unless both are connected, the current does not flow.

Back to our pentagram ritual. As I mentioned before, there are many variations on the basic pentagram rite. The most famous is that used by the Golden Dawn magical order, but my personal feeling is that it is now a little outdated. Crowley has written two variations on the pentagram theme: The Star Ruby and Liber Reguli. These are both excellent pentagram rituals, but are probably a bit complicated for the beginner to learn easily. My favorite pentagram rite is one I devised myself several years ago with the help of my friend Frater Impecunius, called the Nu-Sphere Ritual. The original intention of the Nu-Sphere was to distill the essence of the pentagram rite, reduce it to its simplest form to make it easy for beginners to learn, but also to keep all its power. Here's the text:

THE NU-SPHERE RITUAL

Stand facing East and form the Cross of Light in the following manner:

Visualize a sphere of brilliant white light above your head. Reach up into the sphere and pull down a stream of light to your forehead; then say:

My god is above me.

Draw the light down through your body, forming a vertical pillar. Touch your genitals and say:

My god is below me.

Touching your right shoulder, say:

My god is to the right of me.

Drawing the light across your body to form a horizontal beam, touch your left shoulder and say:

My god is to the left of me.

Cross your arms over your breast (right arm over left) and say:

My god is within me.

Fling your arms upward and outward above your head to form a V shape, and say:

There is no god where I am.

This forms the Cross of Light.

Advance to the Eastern quarter and draw a large upright pentagram in the air before you. Then stand in the sign of the Enterer, arms outstretched in front of you, left foot slightly advanced. Visualize energy streaming from your hands into the pentagram, and vibrate the word:

THERION

Withdraw your arms in the sign of Silence (thumb pressed to your lips, feet together).

Turning to your left, moving widdershins (counterclockwise), repeat this procedure of drawing the pentagram in each of the Northern, Western, and Southern quarters.

When you make the pentagram in the North, vibrate the word:

NUIT

In the West, the word:

BABALON

In the South, the word:

HADIT

Return to the center of the circle and, facing East once more, stretch out your arms to each side. Say:

**Before me the Powers of Earth
Behind me the Powers of Water
On my right hand the Powers of Fire
On my left hand the Powers of Air.**

Visualize the body of the Goddess Nuit arched above your feet in the North, hands in the South, filling the circle with starlight. Invoke with the words:

**Around me burn the stars of Nuit.
And within me burns the star of Hadit.**

Repeat the Cross of Light (first part).

* * *

The first thing to look at when approaching any ritual for the first time is its overall "shape" or structure. Most rituals are primarily symmetrical in shape, and you can see that in the pentagram rite we begin with a Cross of Light section, go to an Invocation section, then finish with another Cross of Light. When we come to do more complicated workings, this symmetrical form will be extended, but we'll come to that in later chapters. Let's look closely at the Cross of Light now.

We begin facing East. East is where the Sun rises, and since the Sun is the source of all energy, it is to the Sun that we will look for our magical energy as well. The Sun also represents the source of our inner energy, the Anahata chakra I mentioned in the last chapter. There are also lines of Earth energy which run along the points of the compass, so aligning yourself in this way can help you to tap into them. If you don't know which way is East, you can use a compass to find out. It is highly unlikely that your temple/bedroom is built directly aligned along an East/West axis, so true East probably lies in a corner somewhere. If so, the best bet is just to take the wall which lies closest to the East as East and keep things simple. Personally, I like my temple to be foursquare, with walls directly in front of, behind, and to each side of me.

In fact "magical East" does not necessarily coincide with magnetic East at all. Thelemic East is the direction of Boleskine, which is near Inverness in Scotland. From Boleskine radiates a very important magical current: it is the Thelemic "Kiblah," the spiritual center of our work. I have frequently been asked "Why the hell is spiritual East in the highlands of Scotland?" Good question. One reason is that this is where Aleister Crowley lived when he first manifested the Thelemic energies in the world, so it was the point from where Thelema really began as a magical force. Think of it as a spring in the Earth from which the Thelemic current flows. All over the world, at all times of the day, Thelemites are directing their rituals to this point, and drawing power from this point. So a good tip is to try to orient the "East" of your temple in this direction if you can, since then you will be able to tap into this flow of power more easily.

If for some reason you are in a situation where you cannot easily determine the direction of magnetic East or Boleskine (if you are staying in a strange house or hotel, for example), the easiest solution of all is to look toward the wall that has the biggest, brightest window, and just call this direction East—remember that East is not so much an absolute direction, but a spiritual direction, the direction that we focus our attention on. The most important thing is: find a direction, call it East and face that way. As soon as you've done this, West is the direction that lies behind you, North is on your left, and South is on your right. At the end of the day, you are the center of your universe, and all these directions depend on you.

To begin the Cross of Light we first visualize bright light above us. This symbolizes the energy which exists outside and above our normal consciousness and which we intend to bring into us. We reach up to this energy and bring it down to us. Those of you who are familiar with Greek mythology may be reminded here of the story of Prometheus, who brought fire from Heaven to Earth, and by so doing, gave humankind the potential to evolve toward godhood. That's exactly the same process that you are doing now, just in a more personal manner.

The first motion is to touch the forehead. The forehead is the position of the Ajna chakra, as I pointed out in chapter 1. Drawing energy down to this chakra helps to make it active and increase your psychic perception. The Ajna is your "third eye," the eye that sees beyond everyday reality. From here you draw the energy down to your genitals, the seat of the Svadisthana chakra, which energizes your creative abilities. After this you draw a line across your shoulders, to balance all your energies into one harmonious whole (think of the way a tightrope walker carries a long pole to help him keep his balance). You then fold your arms across your breast, where the Anahata chakra, seat of the solar energies, lies. This position, arms folded across the chest, right arm over left arm, is known as the sign of Osiris Risen and represents the death of your "normal" consciousness and the rebirth of your "magical" consciousness.

Notice that in the first four movements you have affirmed that your god (whoever it may be) lies all around you in the universe, everywhere outside you. In this fifth sign you are affirming that your god is within you, that you are part of your god and that your god is part of you. The sixth movement is to fling your arms upward and outward, crying, "There is no God where I am." At first sight this phrase seems to contradict everything you have done before, but this is not so. We are now at a very important difference between magick and conventional religion. Conventional religious systems preach that mankind can never know God except indirectly, through prayer or contemplation, but Thelema says that we can *become* God, by directly communicating with the essence of God. In the fifth movement of the Cross of Light, you have affirmed that God is within you, that you are a part of God. Thus you have become God for yourself, and no longer is there a god outside of you. You have achieved "Gnosis": the knowledge of your own divinity. So the sixth movement proclaims that you have destroyed God—in the sense that you have destroyed the illusion that you are separate from God— "There is no God where I am"—there is only one self, undivided from the universe.

This is basically the entire process of invocation in miniature:

    1st: You call ON god
    2nd: You call IN god
    3rd: You ARE god

Once that identification is complete you are in a position to perform your magick, since you are no longer bound by your own limitations as a human. Keep this process in mind—it forms the basis of just about all the active magick that you'll be doing in the future.

As a sideline to this, if you have had a traditional Christian upbringing, you may have noticed that you draw the horizontal bar of the Cross of Light from right to left, instead of the "normal" left to right. This is because here you are the priest and god, not a simple worshipper, so you see the cross from the other side, as it were.

The central section of the pentagram rite is divided into two parts: the banishing of the quarters and the invocation proper. We are now going to create a magick circle. Why a circle? Because the circle is the most balanced of all geometrical forms, and we desire to define a space in which to work. The magick circle is the area where the magician is totally in control—there is nothing in the circle except the energies that you will call in. For convenience we divide the circle into four quarters, corresponding to the four points of the compass, East, North, West, and South.

You are already facing East, and this is where you begin your banishings. The first thing to do is to draw a large five-pointed star, or pentagram, in the air in front of you. (Now you know why this is called the pentagram ritual.) This pentagram represents the five basic elements of existence—Earth, Air, Water, Fire, and Spirit. When you draw pentagrams in the four quarters, you put up a barrier to keep out unwanted forces and also to act as a gateway to channel the forces that you do want. Think of it as a filter, or valve, for magical energy, under your control.

So how do you draw the pentagrams? There are actually several different types of pentagram, each drawn differently, but for this ritual we only need one. This is the Banishing Pentagram of Earth, used as a sort of "general-purpose" pentagram. It's an upright pentagram, which means that it has one point at the top, two points at the bottom. Here's how to do it:

Start by standing upright, feet together, hands loosely by your sides. Bring your dominant (or "writing") hand down to your left side at about the level of your hip, about half a meter in front of your body. Keep your arm fairly straight and rigid all the way through the next movements. Clench the fingers of your hand into a fist then place your thumb between the first and second fingers so that it protrudes slightly: you will use it to draw the pentagram. Now bring your hand up in a straight diagonal line, keeping it about half a meter away, to draw the top center point, which should be directly in front of your face, slightly above your eye level. From here bring your hand down to the level of your right hip. You should have now drawn an upside-down "V" shape in the air in front of you. Now bring your hand across your chest to the level of your left shoulder. Form the horizontal line of the pentagram by bringing your hand directly across your chest, so that it reaches beyond your right shoulder. Complete the pentagram by bringing your hand back down to your left hip.

Don't worry if your first couple of tries are a bit wobbly, that's natural; remember that the instructions above are only approximate. Practice a few times until you can draw a pentagram to be proud of.

When you draw the pentagram, try to imagine it as being made of fire or glowing energy—make it seem as real as you can. After some practice, you should start to see it shimmering faintly even without making a conscious effort.

Now that you have drawn the pentagram, you need to energize it. This is done using a Word of Power and a Sign, or gesture. Words of Power serve an extremely important function in magick ritual, but many beginners find it difficult to understand how a particular word can have power built into it.

In one sense, all words are Words of Power, because it is through our language that we communicate our ideas and desires, but some words do have more power over us than others. Think of the word "mother" for example. This one word contains emotions and connotations that can take weeks or months to express in any other way. And for each person this word has different connotations. Words are packets of information, ideas encapsulated. Magical Words of Power are similarly words which contain many different magical ideas wrapped up in one package. Think of a magick word as a formula, like an equation in mathematics or an atomic formula in chemistry. H_2O means little to someone with no knowledge of science, but when you know what the formula represents, it clearly expresses not only the concept "water," but also how water itself comes into being. So it is with Words of Power. Each word contains an entire magical concept within it, and when you speak these words, you release that power.

The words we will use to energize the pentagram are names of various important Thelemic deities. For now don't worry about what they mean, we'll come to that soon enough. When you speak one of these names, try to put all of your force behind it—don't just mumble it quietly, but pronounce it slowly and carefully. You don't so much say the word, more like "vibrate" it.

If you have ever talked to someone who speaks Spanish or French, you will know how much stronger words can be when they are accompanied by an appropriate gesture (try driving in Paris or Mexico City for a practical demonstration of this). So it is in magick. When you vibrate your Word of Power, you make the sign of the Enterer, the sign of the god Horus.

You are standing facing East, your arms loosely by your sides. With your left foot, take a short step forward, keeping your right foot where it is. As you do this, bring your arms upward and outward from your body until they are straight out in front of you, and lean forward slightly. Then vibrate THERION. As you say the word, feel the force being transmitted along your outstretched arms, through your fingertips, and into the pentagram before you, filling it with energy.

Now slowly bring your left foot back and let your arms fall to the sides. Then bring your dominant hand up to your face and touch your lips with your thumb, like a baby sucking his thumb. This is the Sign of Silence, the gesture of the god Harpocrates (yes, just like Harpo Marx). The sign of the Enterer starts the transmission of energy and the sign of Silence stops the transmission. *Always* follow the sign of the Enterer with the sign of Silence when you do this ritual, otherwise you'll be transmitting energy for hours if you're not careful, and we certainly don't want that to happen.

Stand for a moment in this sign and visualize your pentagram filled with glowing energy in front of you. You will probably find that keeping your eyes closed helps you to visualize better; you see it with your "inner eye."

Now you are finished banishing the Eastern quarter. Turn widdershins (counterclockwise, to your left) so that you are facing North, and draw your second pentagram, energizing it with NUIT. Do the same in the West with the name BABALON, and in the South with HADIT; then turn once more to the East. Note that you go around the circle in a counterclockwise direction because you are banishing, clearing the environment of outside energies. During rituals of invocation, or calling in of energy, you move in the opposite direction, clockwise, called deosil by magicians. Neither direction is better or worse than the other; it is just that they have different qualities. We move widdershins when we wish to clear the circle of influences which we don't want; we move deosil to call in forces that we do want.

Moving widdershins means that you are moving through the elements from Earth, to Air, to Water, to Fire, that is, from the most material element to the most fine. There is a fifth element (the top point of the pentagram) which is the element of Spirit. The element of Spirit is not manifested in the world outside you, it lies within you, and when you move back to the center of the circle and form the cross, you are showing this. The cross also has five points, the four arms and the center point where they meet. This center point is also the point of Spirit. "My God is within me"—remember? Moving from Earth to Spirit shows your Will to aspire beyond earthy existence to achieve contact with spiritual energies.

Not only have you formed a vertical cross in your own body during the Cross of Light section, you have also now formed a horizontal cross within the circle, a cross of pentagrams, front, back, right, and left, with yourself standing at the intersection. This idea of crosses and circles you will find to be a recurring theme in much of the Thelemic magick you will meet in the future. The figure of the cross within the circle is an important and powerful symbol, representing Spirit manifested in Matter, divine energy bonded with the Earth.

Now that you have banished the quarters, you will affirm your magical intention. To do this, slowly raise your arms upward and out to the side of your body, stretching out to form a cross, your hands pointing South and North. You have cleared a space in which to work, and your magick circle represents everything that is you, with the rest of the universe lying outside the circle's boundary. Now you want to draw around your circle the forces that will help you to achieve your aim. The Eastern quarter of the circle is attributed to the element of Earth, so imagine that in front of you lies the whole panoply of nature, verdant green fields, trees and flowers, bursting with new life, filled with the warmth and energy of the Sun. The Western quarter behind you is attributed to the element of Water, so here you will perhaps visualize a waterfall, with flowing, sparkling clear cool water. On your right are the Powers of Fire, so here see and feel a roaring red-hot fire burning your cheek. On your left lie the Powers of Air, and here you can sense the blue sky and the cold winds blowing from the far end of the world, reaching up toward the universe outside. Now visualize this universe outside as infinite space, the night sky filled with glowing starlight. This is the image of the goddess Nuit, the cosmic Isis, the mother of all things. Imagine her body stretched over you, covering and protecting the circle. Say the words:

Around me burn the stars of Nuit.

The pentagrams you have drawn around the circle are, of course, the stars in the body of the goddess Nuit, so you should feel them glow slightly as you say this.

Now imagine that inside you, burning on your breast, is a six-pointed star, the symbol of your magical aspiration, your striving to attain knowledge and power. Say:

And within me burns the star of Hadit.

Hadit is the god of the energy that flames inside you.

The central part of the ritual is now complete. To preserve the symmetrical structure, repeat the Cross of Light, just as you did it at the beginning. Congratulations! You've just done your first pentagram ritual!

* * *

You may have noticed on going through this ritual that you have been asked several times to imagine something, or visualize something. Visualization, or using the power of your imagination creatively, is a very important part of magick. We are generally brought up in this society to "look down" on the imagination; imagination is somehow thus removed from reality and not very useful in daily life. Nothing could be further from the truth. I have often heard people say, "Oh, it's just imagination."

Just imagination! The imagination is the most powerful faculty we possess. We are taught to believe that there is only one "real" reality and that the imagination is removed from that reality; but everything that human beings have created in the world existed first only in the imagination of one person. In order to create something in this outer reality, it first must take form in your own inner reality, then be made material through the application of your Will.

As magicians, we desire to change reality by the use of our rituals. Remember that reality is not a fixed, unchanging object, but rather it is a fluid, continually changing process. When we perform magick, we take hold of reality and sculpt it in the way that we desire; we divert the course of reality's flow, like building a dam in a river.

Of course, ultimately there are as many realities as there are stars in the sky since every person carries their own personal reality around in their head all the time. Reality only exists in your imagination in the first place, so when you change the way you see things, you change reality itself. However, the imagination is a subtle and complex thing. It works by very different rules than the rest of your mind. Whereas your conscious mind works by language and logic, your imagination works with symbols, connected in ways that may often seem illogical.

When you visualize your pentagrams in the air before you, they may be "only" part of your imagination, but the forces and ideas that they symbolize are very real indeed. Those forces are not very useful to you as long as they are only internal. You must externalize your inner energies, so that your Will can be done in the universe outside you. So endeavor to make your visualizations as vivid and as "real" as possible. The more powerful your visualizations, the more effective your magick will be.

The most important thing to remember is that it is no good reading the pentagram ritual and thinking to yourself: "Hmm, quite interesting." You must perform it, and not just once or twice, but as often as you possibly can—this means every day if possible. You need to learn the words and actions by heart, so that they spring naturally to you at any moment. Yes, I know, learning stuff by rote can be a real pain in the ass, but believe me, it pays off! Work this ritual again and again, make it a part of your everyday existence—it is the foundation stone of all the magical ritual work that you will do in the future.

Note: As I mentioned near the beginning of this chapter, the Lesser Banishing Ritual of the Pentagram has gone through many versions and revisions and currently exists in several different forms, each with slightly differing ideas implicit within it. The most common form used in the past has been the Golden Dawn version (given in the back of this book), which differs significantly from the Nu-Sphere in that East is the quarter of Air and North is the quarter of Earth and in that the magician moves around the circle deosil, not widdershins. Although this early version is very effective and has been used by thousands of magicians for a century now, it is based on magical ideas from the pre-Thelemic period (i.e., before 1904). Thelemic magick generally uses the newer attributions that I have given in the Nu-Sphere Rite, and I strongly advise readers who wish to seriously follow the Thelemic path to use these more modern attributions.

FURTHER STUDY

Magick—Part III, Chapter 13: Of the Banishings
Magick—Appendix VI: Liber V vel Reguli
Magick—Appendix VI: The Star Ruby
Magick—Appendix VII: Liber O vel Manus et Sagittae

CHAPTER THREE

THELEMIC COSMOLOGY

While performing the Nu-Sphere ritual, you will have noticed that you were calling on the energies of different gods and goddesses. You probably found this a little strange if you have never performed magick before. Most people in Western societies have been brought up to believe that there can be only one god, and you can either believe that he is all-seeing and all-powerful or that he does not exist at all. The Thelemic magician approaches things differently For the magician, gods and goddesses are basically gigantic forces which contain various universal powers within them. So why do we refer to these forces as gods and goddesses? Quite simply because it's a lot easier to communicate with something that looks and feels like a person, than to communicate with a law of nature. Now someone with a very academic, scientific background might argue with this and say they can relate to a theory as easily as a person, but when all's said and done, you still can't have sex with an equation.

To most people who have grown up in the last thirty years or so, the idea of believing in all these assorted gods is very strange. In some ways this very strangeness can be useful, but at times, especially at the beginning of your magical career, it can make things a little difficult.

"Do gods really exist?" is a question I have heard very, very frequently indeed. The best answer I can give to this is that, quite honestly, I don't know, but the universe behaves as if they do. In other words if you invoke a god or goddess, you will get a result, so for all practical purposes you should assume that they do exist. If you still find this difficult, look at ritual as a form of shared fantasy experience, and act accordingly—after all, when you see someone die in a movie, you don't think "Oh, well, it's just an actor, so it doesn't mean anything"—you suspend your disbelief for the ninety

minutes of the movie in order for the story to stay meaning-
ful, so do the same during the times of your magical work.

The principal gods and goddesses we use in the Thelemic
tradition are drawn from the Egyptian tradition, though since
Thelema is a belief system that draws the best from many different magical cultures, we can effectively use divinities of
many differing types if we desire. Widely differing cultures
have gods who have very similar functions—the Egyptian
god Tahuti (Thoth) is close to the Greek god Hermes and the
Roman god Mercury, for example. For now, we will concentrate only the principal deities of Thelemic magick.

If you look at the picture of the Stele of Revealing on
page 35 you can see the traditional representations of the
major Thelemic deities. If you have a copy of the tarot cards
designed by Aleister Crowley and Lady Frieda Harris, you
can also flick through the pack until you find the trump card
(or "Atu") numbered XX (twenty in Roman numerals). This
card is called The Aeon, and on it you can see another version
of this Stele. The Stele of Revealing is a very important part
of Thelemic ritual. It is a talisman which acts as a gateway for
the current of Thelemic magical energy to manifest in this
world. Meditate on it carefully. All Thelemic temples should
have a reproduction of this Stele set up in the Eastern quarter,
on an altar or on the wall. If you are really dedicated, you can
buy full-size copies of the original Stele in most occult supply
stores (or you can paint one for yourself), but probably the
easiest thing is simply to photocopy the version in this book
or download an electronic reproduction from the Internet. If
you are traveling, carry a tarot pack with you and set up The
Aeon card in the East.

The ultimate god to a Thelemite is in fact a goddess—the
goddess Nuit. Nuit is the Goddess of Infinite Space and is
symbolized as a naked female form, whose body is composed
of the night sky arched over the surface of the Earth. Nuit is
the goddess from whom the whole world springs; she is the
Great Mother of all things that have been, are now, and are

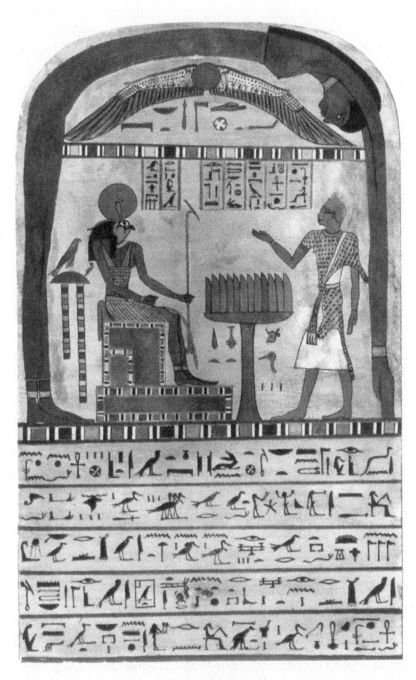

STELE OF REVEALING

to come. Our souls are stars within her body, and thus the symbol of Nuit is the pentagram, the flaming star. *All* magick, in a sense, should be dedicated to Nuit, since she contains all possibilities. All Thelemites should try to spend time contemplating the night sky, for in this way we can come closer to the source of what we are. In the words of that great devotee of Nuit, the astronomer Carl Sagan: "We are made of star-stuff."

In the Stele of Revealing, Nuit is depicted in her classic posture, arching over the top of the frame, since she is the night sky that surrounds all things. You can see her more clearly in a slightly different aspect in the Tarot Atu XVII, The Star, and it will be useful to spend some time carefully studying these depictions. Try to bring the goddess to life, see her giving birth to all things in our universe and feel her love and beauty drawing you to her.

The second principal god we shall deal with is the god Hadit, the consort and complement of Nuit. Where Nuit is potential, Hadit is manifestation; where Nuit is matter, Hadit is motion; where Nuit is Space, Hadit is Time. Nuit is infinitely huge, Hadit infinitely small. Hadit is all the movement and energy of the universe—think of the amount of power released in an atomic reactor, and you will begin to comprehend how much magical force is hidden in the tiniest particles of our universe. But this energy is not only inside inert matter, it is also inside each of us as well. Hadit is "the flame that burns in every heart of man, and in the core of every star." Whereas Nuit can be worshipped by gazing at the night sky, Hadit cannot really be worshipped at all, since he is the god who inspires us to worship in the first place. When you worship Nuit, the sense of awe and wonderment that courses through your body is the power of Hadit rising within you. You cannot worship Hadit, because he is not outside you to be worshipped. He is within you and fills your being when you perform your magick—you do not worship Hadit, you *are* Hadit. Because of this Hadit is portrayed as a glowing ball of energy with wings, and one of his symbols is the six-pointed star, two triangles interlaced, the union of man and god.

If you look again at the Stele of Revealing, you can see Hadit near the top, a winged globe of fire, rushing upward toward the body of Nuit. The child of Nuit and Hadit is the god Horus, or to call him by one of his full names, Ra-Hoor-Khuit. Ra-Hoor-Khuit is portrayed as having the body of a tall, strong man with the head of a hawk and is the figure who contains the active energies of Thelemic magick within him. He is associated with the Sun and with the powers of the Air and all fiery things. To use a more earthy metaphor, he is a god who really kicks ass—the Dirty Harry of the Thelemic pantheon, and like Dirty Harry he has no time for society's traditional moral values. Conquest and success are enough. Many people brought up in Western "Christian" cultures find it difficult to identify with the destructive aspects of this god's character, but they are essential, since in order to create something new, one must destroy the old. To make the paper for this book meant destroying a tree—did you realize that you had caused the death of a living creature when you bought it?

Change implies the destruction of the old to make way for the new, and the one constant in life is change. You are destroying your own personality right now as you read (hopefully). Why hopefully? Because if you were completely satisfied with yourself the way you are now, you wouldn't be reading this in the first place, since this book is about transformation of the self. To transform yourself properly takes courage and, dare I say it, ruthlessness. You must be willing to cut away the ineffective parts of yourself, burn them up in the fire of your aspiration, and use the flames to bring new light into your life. That is the power and the path of Ra-Hoor-Khuit and of the Thelemic way.

Looking once again at the Stele of Revealing, you can see that Ra-Hoor-Khuit is the central figure of the Stele, as he is the central figure of all our magical energies. He is throned, to symbolize his rule over this time, and carries a wand, to show that he is active in wielding his power.

Facing Ra-Hoor-Khuit in the Stele is a human figure dressed in a leopard skin, the traditional garb of a priest of Egypt. This figure is Ankh-af-na-khonsu, an earlier incarnation of Aleister Crowley, but in a more general sense he represents all aspirants, all magicians who work with the Thelemic magical current. You will notice that the head of this priest is on the same level as that of the god Ra-Hoor-Khuit. This is very important. In the pictures showing the relation of gods and mankind in most other belief systems, you can see that the god is always shown to be above the priest, who is normally down on his knees looking up and begging for divine mercy. Thelemic magicians do not kneel and beg. We approach our gods as equals; we talk to them directly but still with respect for their knowledge and power. We do not fear our gods; we live in their presence.

Ra-Hoor-Khuit holds a very special position for Thelemites, since he is the god particularly responsible for overseeing humanity's development at this period of time, a time commonly referred to by Thelemic magicians as the Aeon of Horus. The magical development of the human race can be split it into several different periods, each lasting many centuries, called Aeons, of which the Aeon of Horus is the third.

In the first period, the Aeon of Isis, religion was matriarchal, based on the mysteries of childbirth. It was not generally understood that sex and reproduction were connected —most primitive humans presumably had difficulty in remembering the dates of random sexual activities for nine months, but they were aware of the connection between pregnancy and menstruation, and the connection between menstruation and the cycles of the moon. Accordingly, female lunar goddesses were the primary divinities worshipped in this age of the Mother.

After many centuries of nomadic hunting and gathering, people discovered agriculture and began to settle, building fixed territories to live in all the time. The male's job changed from hunting for food to protecting the lands and the livestock. Tribes became bigger and more organized, forming kingdoms and nations. Men finally figured out that they too had something to do with reproducing the species, and the entire balance of human society changed into a patriarchal system. No longer were the lunar goddesses revered as the supreme deities. The Sun was more important now, for it was he who ripened the crops in the fields that kept the tribe alive. The Sun was a mighty and terrible god, who rose over the world in his strength every morning and died every night. Religion became solar in nature, with the mysteries of death and rebirth forming its ceremonies. Many of the major religions of today are from this Aeon, called the Aeon of Osiris, the age of the Father. The myth of Jesus dying on the cross and being reborn again is a very obvious example of a sun-based religious teaching.

The Aeon of Osiris continued until around the beginning of this century, until 1904 (common year); then it was superseded by the Aeon of Horus, the age of the Child. We now know that the Sun does not die every night, but that it lives all the time and its death is but an illusion. Birth and death are parts of one continuous process of eternal Being. The Aeon of Horus is the Aeon in which the formula of religion is Life. As Thelemic magicians we know that we are immortal souls—"Every man and every woman is a star."

It is Ra-Hoor-Khuit who speaks in the third chapter of Liber AL, usually considered to be the most difficult of the three chapters to understand. Many newcomers to the Thelemic way, especially those brought up in a pampered First World lifestyle, find this chapter of Liber AL very brutal and violent. They are right: it *is* brutal and violent, but so is the world that we inhabit, and if we wish to live up to our fullest potential, we must be capable of dealing with that brutality. Thelema is not a religion which provides a comfortable means of escape from the problems of the world; it is a religion which provides a method for us to live totally within the world, to cope with its difficulties, to overcome them, and, most important, to change the world to make it a better place to live in. To do all these things, we need the power and energy of our Lord, Ra-Hoor-Khuit. Yet though his power is the power of the Sun, hard, bright, shining, like the blade of a sword, it is also the power that warms us, gives us all our life and light. Ra-Hoor-Khuit may be a warrior god, but he is above all the god of eternal life. He brings to us the utter joy of being alive, of being part of the wild and carefree dance of the universe, free, unique, and individual, unfettered by fear or tribulation. With Ra-Hoor-Khuit by our side, we walk through the world knowing always that our Will is triumphant, that we have the capability to do and be whatever our heart truly desires.

The fourth of the great Thelemic divinities is the god Hoor-paar-kraat, more commonly known by the English version of his name, Harpocrates. You will recall that we briefly encountered this god before during the Nu-Sphere rite. Hoor-paar-kraat is the brother of Ra-Hoor-Khuit, and whereas Ra-Hoor-Khuit is the outflowing of energy and power, Hoor-paar-kraat is energy contained within and the god of silence and inner strength. He is represented as a child, usually sitting on a lotus flower sucking his thumb, just like a baby does. The tarot card most associated with Hoor-paar-kraat is Atu 0, The Fool, though you can also see a more traditional representation of him in Atu XX, The Aeon, where he is shown "invisible." He is not shown on the Stele of Revealing.

Hoor-paar-kraat, being the God of Silence, does not have a chapter in Liber AL of his own; however, the entire book was dictated to Aleister Crowley by Aiwass, who is the Minister of Hoor-paar-kraat, charged with the job of communicating the wishes of the god. Hoor-paar-kraat is a god who is particularly close to those who would aspire to be Thelemic magicians, and is it very worthwhile for all aspirants to learn to draw on the strength of this god. The easiest and quickest way to do this is by a technique called the Assumption of God-forms. All gods have particular postures, gestures, clothing, etc., associated with them and by, in a

HOOR-PAAR-KRAAT

sense, imitating these features, the magician can also partici-pate in the power of the god. The assumption of the god-form of Hoor-paar-kraat is one of the simplest to achieve.

Read the description of Hoor-paar-kraat above carefully and memorize it. Study the tarot cards which feature Hoor-paar-kraat, and while so doing, try to take in not only what the god looks like, but also the "atmosphere" or aura which surrounds him. If you can, get hold of a book on Egyptian mythology and study his pictures, or better still, go to a museum that has an Egyptian room and study him there. If you are lucky enough to be able to visit London or Berlin, make the Egyptian museum collections there your absolute number one priority.

Now you are ready to begin assuming the god-form of Hoor-paar-kraat. First sit in your chosen asana, that by now you should have been practicing regularly (but probably haven't if, like me, you're too impatient and would rather read the whole book at one go than start working). Close your eyes, and breathe slowly and deeply. Raise your thumb and press it lightly between your lips. Begin to visualize your body as that of a young boy-child, naked. Your hair curls around one ear (it can help to do this in reality before you begin, if your hair is long enough). You are sitting on a large lotus flower, which in turn floats gently on the surface of a large river. This river is the Nile, source of the land's fertility. On the banks you can see pyramids, illuminated by strong sunlight, which you can feel beating down upon you, filling your body with heat and life. Down in the depths of the Nile lurk crocodiles, snapping at you, but they cannot harm you at all, for you are protected from all things by a shining blue-black egg which surrounds and envelops your whole body. This is the Egg of Spirit, and it is dark, as it absorbs all energy from outside and keeps your own energies stored up within you, ready for when they are needed. You are a babe, a baby in the womb of our All-Mother Nuit, secure in the knowledge that she will guide and protect you. Sit in your asana for a few minutes, feeling the energies of Hoor-paar-kraat build up within you, feeling your aura being strengthened to protect you from any harm that may lie ahead in the next days. Then, when you feel the time is right, slowly become aware of yourself fully again, back in your own body, back in this world. Now clap your hands together, hard. The sound of the clapping, plus the stinging sensation in your palms, will help to bring you back to earth. Stand up now, and stamp your feet on the ground a few times. That's it, you've just invoked a Thelemic God!

This may seem a very simple ritual, and it is; however, it is a very, very useful one for the beginning Thelemite, as it provides relaxation, concentration, visualization, protection, and magical strength, all in one convenient take-home package. Use it regularly. Your magical energy will increase more and more if you invoke often. As I keep emphasizing, regular practice builds up magical power—the more you do it, the stronger it gets. So perform this assumption as often as you can. When you feel confident enough, you can add it to your daily yoga practice—it will give increased depth to all that you have been doing before.

There are two other Thelemic deities mentioned in the Nu-Sphere rite, but who are not part of ancient Egyptian mythology: these are Therion and Babalon. They are not shown on the Stele of Revealing, but are portrayed in the tarot on Atu XI, Lust. These two are not as "cosmic" as the previous deities mentioned in this chapter, rather they are more down to earth counterparts.

Babalon is the goddess shown on the Lust card, the goddess of all pleasure. She is known as the Virgin Whore: whore because she accepts and contains all things; virgin because she always retains her inner purity. She shows that Thelemites should endeavor not to close themselves off from the outside world, from the ideas and feelings of others, but should attempt to unite with others through the power of love. She carries the Holy Graal in her hand, the cup which contains the "blood of the Saints," the accumulated power of all who perform her magick. We can drink from that cup and thus partake of the energies of Thelema.

The beast that Babalon rides upon is Therion (Therion literally means "beast" in Greek). Therion is the untrammeled force of nature, the strength and potency of the wild animal within us. He is also closely connected with the Sun, since the Sun is the source of nature's power. He is many-headed to show that he manifests in many ways, through sexuality, through violence, through hunger, through all intensity of the body's desire.

Babalon rides upon the Therion showing love travels on the back of desire, that the body supports the spirit. Both of them are very physical deities. In opposition to the religions of the last centuries which taught that the body was unclean, sinful, and needs to be purified to gain redemption, we Thelemites generally believe that the body's desires are pure and holy, that these desires are what keep us alive and vibrant. Meditate on these deities, understand how they relate to yourself, experience their energy in your daily life. They only really live when you let them live within you.

FURTHER STUDY

Magick Appendix VII: Liber O vel Manus et Sagittae (part III)
Magick Without Tears—Chapter 36: Quo Stet Olympus
Magick Without Tears—Chapter 76: The Gods

CHAPTER FOUR

More Yoga:
Pranayama and Mantrayoga

In chapter 1 we started with some basic yoga techniques, and then in chapters 2 and 3, we moved through various other aspects of the Thelemic path. In this chapter we are going to expand on those preliminary yoga exercises.

Breath is Life. This is one of those facts that is so simple and obvious that we forget just how vital it really is. When we breathe, we affirm our lives, our Will to survive, our place in the Universe. In your first yoga exercises, you learned to concentrate on your breath, to become aware of the primary process by which you live. Now it is time to go one step further and actually begin to control your breathing, and by doing so, begin to actively change your life at its most fundamental level.

This control of breathing is technically known as pranayama. The word "prana" has no real equivalent term in conventional English (like so many of the terms used in the world of magick—unfortunately...). Prana basically means the life energy which exists in the air and which we take into ourselves with every breath. Through pranayama we can learn how to increase the intake of prana and how to improve its flow through our organism. Thus through pranayama we increase the total energy that we have available for our use.

As you have performed the first asanas and begun to concentrate on your breathing, you will probably have found that your breathing has naturally slowed down and become somewhat deeper and more relaxed. If not, don't worry about it, for each person has their own speed and rhythm. Note the use of the word "naturally" just now. Most of us do not breathe at all naturally; we breathe shallowly and without proper rhythm. The reasons for this are deep ones, but simply put our breathing is a reflection of the psychological complexes we have built up throughout our earlier life. A good exercise to try over the next few days is to observe your friends and workmates closely and watch how they breathe. You will soon notice that those with problems of confidence, or with sexual problems, tend to breathe very shallowly and will often hunch over, shoulders angled forward, constricting their lung capacity. Their lives will often be as shallow as their breathing. Conversely, those who have a capacity for experiencing life to the fullest will tend to breathe deeply, laugh with their whole body. So you will see that simply controlling your breathing can revolutionize your entire approach to living.

So how do we go about this revolution? First, get back into your chosen asana. Now I want you to begin counting, a beat of four, like the average rock 'n' roll song: 1, 2, 3, 4— not too fast, please (we're not doing speed metal here). We use a count of four, since four is the number of the material world, of stability. During the first count of four I want you to breathe in, then for the next count of four breathe out, then breathe in for four again, and so on. Try to count at a speed which makes breathing reasonably comfortable, but remember to try also to keep it fairly slow and steady. Once you have found a rhythm that suits you, keep it regular and fit your breathing to it.

The previous exercise should not be too difficult, but practice it a few times to get to understand how to control your breath. When you feel reasonably confident, you can begin to extend the practice a little. First try to breathe out for twice as long as you breathe in: that is, breathe in for one count of four, then breathe out for two counts of four. This may be slightly more difficult at first, but will become much more natural as time goes on. When you have mastered this, you can go on even further, by adding a period of rest between inbreath and outbreath. Breathe in for a count of four as before, but this time hold the breath in for another count of four, then breathe out for two counts of four. You will probably find this to be quite difficult, but persevere. This "four times four" rhythm forms the basis of pranayama (as it also forms the basis of very many other things in magick).

You may find your heart begins to beat faster while you do this exercise, as your body attempts to use the extra oxygen that you are taking in. If so, try slowing down your counting rhythm until your heart is beating slowly and calmly. This may take a few days or more of work until you get it right.

If you practice the preceding exercise, you may well notice an interesting phenomenon occurring. After you have been repeating the numbers 1-2-3-4 for a few minutes, they seem to lose something of their meaning and become hypnotic. Try this experiment now. Pick a word at random, any word (you can use a book, just open it at any page and pick the first word your eye lights upon). Now begin to repeat the word, at first out loud, then silently. Keep repeating it over and over again, without stopping. Keep this up for at least fifteen minutes. The word will begin to seem very strange to you. As you keep repeating it, it will pass through different stages of meaning (or non-meaning) to you. There are various theories as to why this should be, but the important thing for our purposes is that this repetition has an extremely interesting effect on the brain and can be used by us to bring about changes in our consciousness. When the repetition is combined with other magical techniques, we have a tool for programming our own thought systems (or, as it has been called by Dr. John Lilly "meta-programming the human bio-computer").

If, instead of just repeating the numbers 1-2-3-4, or any word at random, we repeat a word or phrase that has a particular significance to us, we can affect our consciousness as well as our bodies during yoga practice. To some, this may be obvious, to others it may be difficult to grasp at first. As usual, the best way to understand something is to practice it, and this practice is called mantra.

A mantra can be composed of any word or phrase repeated over a period of time and used as a metaprogramming tool. This has led some people into the classical error of assuming that if you pick a sentence such as "Every day, in every way I get better and better," and repeat it often enough, then you will *get* better and better. You *might*, but I doubt it very much. All you will have done is convince part of your consciousness that you have become "better" (whatever that means), while managing to confuse the rest of your consciousness, which is quite aware that you have stayed exactly the same all the time (consciousness is *complicated*, never forget this!). In fact, essentially what you will have done is to bring about a form of mild schizophrenia in yourself.

The best thing, especially as you are just beginning, is to use common mantras that have been around for a while and have a proven track record of effectiveness. Choosing a mantra is not unlike the process of choosing an asana that we went through at the beginning of our yoga training. There are many mantras for many purposes, but for now the best bet is to choose one for general purposes and stick to it. For our purposes, the mantra is best if it is reasonably short so that it is easy to remember and fairly rhythmical so that we can use it to time our 4 x 4 breathing pattern. Personally, I also think that it is good when a mantra is in a strange language, as this strangeness helps us to warp our minds out into the foreign magical realms that we wish to explore.

One of the oldest, and to my mind, still one of the best yoga mantras is the classic "Aum mani padme hum." This literally means "Hail, jewel in the lotus," and since the god Hoor-paar-kraat is pictured as sitting on a lotus flower (as you know from the exercise introduced in chapter 3), this mantra is particularly suitable to our work. The mantra is pronounced "Aum ma-ni pad-me hum." If you set up a rhythm of four beats to a bar, our 1-2-3-4 breathing rhythm, and chant this mantra, you should see that it will fit perfectly.

An even simpler mantra is "Aum Tat Sat Aum." If you can't recite this one, then there's really no hope for you! Personally, I find this one a touch too simple, but it might be just the one you need.

Another mantra that you might like to try is "Aum nama shivaya, Shivaya nama Aum," which also adapts itself very well to a 4 x 4 rhythm (Aum na-ma shi-va-ya, Shi-va-ya na-ma Aum). It is a little more complicated than the other examples above, but still not too hard. This mantra refers to the god Shiva, the creator/destroyer god of Hindu mythology, who is a patron god of magicians. There are many other possibilities. Crowley gives a good selection in Magick, and you can find many more in other yoga books. However, for our purposes I recommend one of the simple ones above. As time goes on you can expand your repertoire when you need to.

At first do not attempt to coordinate your breathing and your mantra. Forget your breathing for a little while and just concentrate on reciting the mantra slowly and regularly. You can chant it out loud to begin with, but after a while let it sink down into quietness—but keep reciting it internally.

When you have tried this exercise a few times, you will notice that your breathing is becoming synchronized to the rhythm of the mantra. You can now begin to concentrate on this and use the mantra to time the regularity of your breathing, just like you used a count of 1-2-3-4 before. Of course, if you are using the mantra as a timing device like this, you will recite it internally—it's quite hard to perform pranayama and talk at the same time!

After a few months of daily practice of pranayama (sometimes in as little as a few weeks), you will find yourself becoming much more aware and relaxed in your daily life as well as in your magical work. One pleasant side effect is that your body's sweat secretions will also begin to change, and you should find that your skin becomes softer and more sweet smelling as a consequence. You also produce more pheromones, making you more sexually attractive—so keep that in mind at any time when you are feeling discouraged!

Another good way to keep up your mantra practice is to recite a mantra while walking. Simply fit each beat of the four-part rhythm to a step, timing your mantra to your walking speed, or vice versa, whichever seems more comfortable. This works in a similar manner to the military mantra of "left, right, left, right" so beloved of drill sergeants the world over. Linking your pace to your mantra helps to drill your mind and has the useful side effect of making long walks seem much shorter. If you don't walk much, take this as encouragement to change this unhealthy state of affairs in your life—it's important that you exercise all the faculties you possess and do not neglect the fundamentals. Walking in the countryside or in the park is a very good way to obtain fresh air and thus increase your intake of vital prana. So consider the act of walking an important part of your pranayama and mantrayoga exercises.

One technique which is associated with pranayama is the vibration of god names. This is a good way of tying together all the previous exercises we have already gone through. Effectively, you perform an Assumption of a God-form like before and use the name of that god as a mantra. In the Hoor-paar-kraat assumption, you should slowly repeat his name over and over again. As you draw in your breath, imagine the name and energy of the god being drawn into your body and down, penetrating your forehead, throat, heart, solar plexus, navel, genitals, and spine (your chakric system). Then, on your outbreath, feel the energy rising up and outward in the reverse manner, until it is spreading out across the universe. Practice of this will not only allow you to passively feel part of the gods, but will allow you to participate in their energies fully. It must always be remembered that gods are not passive statues, but living, breathing entities. Gods are not *things*, they are *processes*.

One mantra which is especially important for Thelemic magicians is the ancient Egyptian invocation from the Stele of Revealing:

**A ku dua
Tuf ur biu
Bi a'a chefu
Dudu ner af an nuteru**

This is much more complicated than the single line mantras given above, but will still fit into a 4 x 4 rhythm (with a little practice). For general meditation purposes it is perhaps a bit much, but it is very good for raising your magical energy, since it is much more "active" in style than the others. If you recite this mantra, you will draw down the Thelemic current into you, charging you with power. It is perhaps particularly suited to the assumption of the god-form of Ra-Hoor-Khuit. A good exercise is to prop up a copy of the Stele of Revealing before you, get into your asana, and meditate on the Stele while reciting this mantra. Through this process you may well find yourself achieving new insights into your magick.

FURTHER STUDY

Magick—Part I, Chapter 2
Magick—Appendix VII: Liber E vel Exercitiorum, Part IV
Magick—Appendix VII: Liber O vel Manus et Sagittae (Part III)
Magick—Appendix VII: Liber RV vel Spiritus
Magick Without Tears—Chapter 25: Fascinations, Invisibility, Levitation, Transmutations, Kinks in Time

CHAPTER FIVE

EVERYDAY MAGICK

By this time in your magical development, you should be seeing real changes beginning to appear in your life, but until now your magical life and your "real" life have been quite separate. In order to become a Thelemic magician in the fullest sense, you must make your whole life magical. As Thelemites we do not only worship our gods on Sunday in church; we see, feel, and touch godhood at every moment of every day. The world is not an evil place for us, a place that we must withdraw from. We do not live as a preparation for "heaven," whatever that might be; we wish to make the world we inhabit into a heaven for ourselves right now.

You will probably already have noticed that most people create their own realities. For someone who really believes that the world is a miserable place, the world is, sure enough, a really miserable place. This is because Mr. Misery's mind screens out all things that might actually make him happy—he has no awareness of most of the good things that are actually happening right in front of his nose. I'm sure that you don't need me to explain this type of person to you; everybody has a Mr. Misery somewhere in their locality. Observe him, see how his vision is limited, and thus his potential for living is diminished also.

Now hear this: *you* are Mr. Misery.

Hard, huh? But it's true. Your vision is extremely limited indeed. You have no real understanding of what the hell is going on around you 90 percent of the time. Don't believe me? OK, explain what happens—in detail—when you turn the ignition key of your car. Or when you turn on the light switch. Or when you put a disk in your hi-fi. Or when you eat a good meal. Or when you look in the eyes of the person you love.

Maybe you're a genius and can explain all of these things—but I said in detail, remember? Did you manage to bring in the quantum interactions at the subatomic level? Do you know what happens even beneath that? No, you don't (or if you do, I'd love to hear from you). And we haven't even started to touch on what happens inside your mind yet—whatever the mind is in the first place.

Well, in reality you *do* know precisely how all these things happen; it's just that the knowledge is buried away in a part of yourself that you are not normally aware of. It now seems highly likely that we are all, all of the time, fully able to perceive what is going on everywhere in the whole universe. There are various theories as to why this might be. According to Dr. Rupert Sheldrake, our consciousness is linked to the consciousness of others by a Morphogenetic Field, which acts to transmit information telepathically between us. (Bell's theorem proves that information is nonlocal, i.e., that information can—indeed must—travel faster than the speed of light.)

All this universal information is "magical"—we cannot know it directly but we can know it by inference; we can feel it inside us. We feel it inside us all the time, but our consciousness is incapable of recognizing what is going on because we are too busy concentrating on "real" life. If you have ever seen a cat outside a mouse hole waiting for its prey to appear, you have some idea what I mean. You can call the cat's name, you can make loud noises, but you won't distract the cat. In fact, the cat will literally not be able to hear—its concentration is so total that its hearing no longer even has a neurological connection to its brain.

So to be a good magician, you must be a magician all the time. You must train yourself to be aware of all the magical things going on around you as you live. The way to do this is by "background concentration." By this I mean that you must train your consciousness to be working and meditating all day long. Everything you do must be a magical affirmation of yourself as a magician. This is not anywhere near as difficult as it might sound.

The first thing you must do is start to become aware of your place in the universe. OK, tell me, right now, where *exactly* you are located in the universe. Hard question to answer? No, not at all. I'll tell you exactly where you are. You are, right now, in the precise center of the universe. Most people are aware that Einstein pointed out that all things in the universe are relative, but very few bother to go one step further and ask what these things are relative to. The universe is relative to the observer—that is, *you*. You are, quite literally, the center of the universe, but you have been brought up to believe that you are only one small unimportant cog in the great machinery of the world. You have been conditioned to think of your place in life as being irrelevant—that political decisions are made for you by politicians, that religious decisions are made for you by priests; you have been taught that your desires and feelings must always be compromised because the moral values which your society has imposed on you are more important than your own personal Will. It's time to change all of that.

When you performed your Banishing Ritual of the Pentagram earlier, you set up a magick circle and surrounded it with stars, with the body of Nuit. By doing so, you were affirming your place at the center of creation, for the magick circle is the symbol of the universe that you inhabit. So let's do a ritual which acts to affirm your being not only every day but several times every day. We also need a ritual that will call energy down into your being to assist you in your work of living from day to day. The source of energy in our world is the Sun, and it is the Sun who marks our day since a day is but the name for the time it takes for the Sun to rise and fall through one complete revolution. So our everyday ritual will consist of hailing the Sun god, in every aspect—as it rises, shines, sets, and leaves us in darkness. The ritual we will use is a slight variation of one written by Aleister Crowley, called Liber Resh (Resh is the Hebrew letter associated with the Sun):

LIBER RESH

Fold your arms across your breast right over left (the sign of Osiris Risen), then perform the appropriate salutation for the time of day:

At dawn, face East, where the Sun is rising, and say:

> **Hail unto thee who art Ra in Thy rising, even unto Thee who art Ra in Thy strength, who travellest over the Heavens in thy bark at the Uprising of the Sun. Tahuti standeth in His splendor at the prow, and Ra-Hoor abideth at the helm. Hail unto Thee from the Abodes of Night!**

At midday, face South, where the Sun is at midpoint, and say:

> **Hail unto thee who art Ahathoor in Thy triumphing, even unto Thee who art Ahathoor in Thy beauty, who travellest over the Heavens in thy bark at the Mid-course of the Sun. Tahuti standeth in His splendor at the prow, and Ra-Hoor abideth at the helm. Hail unto Thee from the Abodes of Morning!**

At sunset, face West where the Sun is setting, and say:

> **Hail unto thee who art Tum in Thy setting, even unto Thee who art Tum in Thy joy, who travellest over the Heavens in thy bark at the Downgoing of the Sun. Tahuti standeth in His splendor at the prow, and Ra-Hoor abideth at the helm. Hail unto Thee from the Abodes of Day!**

At midnight, face North, where the Sun is at its weakest, and say:

Hail unto thee who art Khephra in Thy hiding, even unto Thee who art Khephra in Thy silence, who travellest over the Heavens in thy bark at the Midnight Hour of the Sun. Tahuti standeth in His splendor at the prow, and Ra-Hoor abideth at the helm. Hail unto Thee from the Abodes of Evening!

After each salutation, stand in the sign of Silence, the sign of Hoor-paar-kraat, thumb to your lips, and feel the power of the Sun flowing through you.

* * *

Oh no, I can hear you cry right now—meditate at *dawn*?!?!?! I don't get up until half past ten! OK, OK, point taken. I'd like to pretend that I am a truly great Holy Guru, but to be honest the number of times I've gotten up at dawn to do this exercise can be counted on the fingers of one hand (maybe two, if I'm not being modest...). I've occasionally been up at dawn while coming home from a club, but that's about it. If you can manage to do each of these salutations at exactly the correct time, you are fantastically wonderful, and you have my compliments but it isn't absolutely necessary—we do have to live in the real world after all, and it can be a little bit difficult to do all of these things precisely when they should be done. The best compromise is to perform the dawn meditation just after you wake up (just before your regular yoga practice is ideal), do the midday one sometime around noon (you *are* awake by then, I assume?), the evening one when the Sun is setting, and the midnight one either at midnight or just before retiring to bed, whichever is better for you. Of course, if you're a night-shift worker, you'll have to work on a slightly different time scale, but it shouldn't be impossible to work out a satisfactory schedule—so no excuses, please!

The important thing is to do all four—just one or two is not enough. A teacher of mine, a Thelemic magician of many years' experience, used to tell his students to do all four salutations first thing in the morning, because that way they would be sure not to forget one. Although this is certainly true, it negates the point of the exercise somewhat, so do try your best to perform all four at times which are approximately close to the four stated in the text of the ritual. It will be much more effective that way.

Note that if you are in the Southern hemisphere, the North/South axis is reversed of course.

You will find that this ritual really does have a huge effect on the way you see life around you. We are so removed from the very basic things which govern our lives—most people never even think about the importance of the Sun in everything we do—and the Sun really *is* important. I had been a Thelemite for years and always ignored this exercise (mainly because I hated the idea of getting out of bed at dawn), but when I finally started performing it, it made an immense difference to my whole perception of my magical work and my place in the world. I cannot stress the importance of this ritual highly enough. It will add immense power and speed to your development if practiced regularly.

NOTES ON LIBER RESH

You will have noticed that we hail the Sun by different names depending on the time of day. The Egyptians had several different gods attributed to the Sun, each one showing a different aspect of the Sun's power—there's a lot of sun in Egypt after all...

The sun in the morning is Ra. We have already met Ra on the Stele of Revealing in his guise of Ra-Hoor-Khuit, so we don't need to say too much more about this aspect here. At midday, the Sun is Ahathoor (sometimes spelled Hathor), who is the goddess of love and beauty, similar to Venus in Roman mythology. At sunset we have Tum (or Atum), the god who is the creator of humankind, and at midnight, Khephra, who is normally shown in the form of a scarab beetle.

This beetle was well known in Egypt for laying its eggs inside a ball of dung, which it pushed around with its foreclaws in the evening. This ball giving birth to new hidden beetles was an appropriate symbol for the Sun lying hidden and dormant before being born anew in the morning.

These gods are described by the two most appropriate characteristics due to their position. Thus Ra is rising and strong; Ahathoor triumphs (attains greatest victory over the darkness) and is beautiful; Tum is setting and joyful (evening is the time when we take our pleasures); and Khephra is hidden and silent (but still there).

The Sun god is described as traveling in a bark, or ship. To the Egyptians, whose civilization was based largely on river travel along the Nile, it was only natural that the Sun god would travel his long journey through the sky by boat—they didn't have rocket ships after all, despite the claims of people like Erich Von Daniken. This bark of the Sun is crewed permanently by two gods. Tahuti (or Thoth), the Egyptian god of Magick, is similar to the Roman god Mercury, and he stands at the prow, looking out ahead, as he represents our magical vision seeing clearly through the day. Tahuti is described as being "in his splendor" as it is through our vision, our creativity, that we shed our light over the world. Ra-Hoor is at the helm, representing the magical Will that guides us straight and steady. He "abideth," for no matter what we may do or think, our Will is always with us, always there to drive us on.

Immediately after performing Liber Resh is a good time to meditate on Hoor-paar-kraat and assume the god-form of him. You might also want to try reciting the mantra from the Stele of Revealing that I mentioned in the last chapter. If you are an initiate of a Thelemic magical Order, such as OTO, you can use the signs that you have been taught at your initiation instead of the basic general purpose signs that I have given here.

**

By now, you should have become used to doing breathing exercises, and you should be beginning to see that your breathing is changing generally, even when you are not practicing yoga. This is good, since, as I pointed out in the last chapter, breath is the foundation of life—it is simply the most important thing that you do. The second most important thing that you do is eating, and it is to this that we will turn our attention next.

No, I'm not going to give you a lesson here on the importance of a macrobiotic diet to a magician. What I am going to show you is the importance of understanding what you are truly doing when you eat.

Why do you eat? Simple question, simple answer—because you are hungry—right? But why do you *eat*? Well, you eat to stay alive, right? So the question, "Why do you eat?" is ultimately identical with the question, "Why do you live?" Well, why do you live? What is the purpose of your life? This is a question that most people think about once or twice a year perhaps, but try not to think about too often, usually because they have no good answer to it. Thelemites realize that this question is the most important that we can ask ourselves, because this is the basis of all that we do. If you don't know what you want, what good will your magical powers be to you?

When Thelemites sit down to eat, we use this as an opportunity to examine ourselves and our motivations. We do this by means of a short ritual, known as "saying Will." It is best if this is performed by two people sitting down together, but you can easily adapt it for solo use.

> 1ST PERSON: Raps the table eleven times with a knife or other suitable implement, in the sequence three taps, then five, then another three (usually written 3-5-3). Then says: **Do what thou wilt shall be the whole of the Law.**
>
> 2ND PERSON: **What is thy Will?**

1ST: **It is my Will to eat and drink.**

2ND: **To what end?**

1ST: **To fortify my body.**

2ND: **To what end?**

1ST: **That I may accomplish the Great Work.**

2ND: **Love is the law, love under will.**

1ST: Gives a single rap, then says: **Fall to.**

Notice the phrase "the Great Work." The Great Work is the end result of all our magick, and since all of us are different, the Great Work will be different for each of us also. Most of us do not yet have a full understanding of what our place in the universe is, so we simply say "the Great Work," and every time that we say it, we strive to comprehend more fully what that Great Work might be for us. As we grow and change in our magical career, our understanding of our Great Work grows too.

This preceding little ritual is very simple, but very useful indeed, and you should try to use it before every meal, if possible, and certainly before your main meal each day. At first it will seem a bit of a chore, but after a while it becomes a habit, until you begin to do it naturally every time you sit down to eat. Do not underestimate the importance of saying Will—in time, the message of self-examination that it sends will penetrate deep into your psyche and will assist you in your quest to find your True Self.

FURTHER STUDY

Magick—Appendix VII: Liber Resh vel Helios
Magick without Tears—Introduction Letter A
Magick Without Tears—Chapter 18: The Importance of Our Conventional Greetings

CHAPTER SIX

THELEMIC MORALITY

If you've gotten this far, you should've been performing Thelemic magick for some time already, but as yet I haven't really described just what Thelema essentially is. This has been intentional, because Thelema is essentially an active system, rather than a passive set of beliefs. Thelema is much better understood by doing, not reading, though ironically most of the Thelemites I know are obsessive bookworms (myself included).

Most books dealing with "New Age" beliefs start off by reassuring you that their system is "NOT A RELIGION!" but some sort of scientific super-psychology. I'm not afraid to admit that Thelema *is* a religion of a sort; however, it is much less of a traditional religion than almost any other belief system (including most so-called "scientific" systems). The motto of Aleister Crowley's famous magical periodical *The Equinox* was: "The method of science, the aim of religion," which I think sums up the Thelemic attitude perfectly. Let's examine just what a religion is anyway.

Most people these days have a bit of a knee-jerk reaction to the word religion, brought on by forced overexposure to such insane beliefs as conventional Christianity and Islam. The word "religion" has been hijacked and debased by the priests of faiths like these, until now it has become a dirty word among most intelligent right-thinking people in the Western world. The word "religion" springs from roots meaning piety: the Latin word *religio*, the opposite idea to *negligens*, negligent, uncaring, unaware. It also springs from a root meaning to join together things that are separate, which in fact is the same meaning as the word "yoga" (compare the English word "yoke," which ties oxen together, for example). So religion is a word which describes the process of becoming aware and unified, of joining together all things which are diverse; it is the union of body and spirit, self and not-self, human and god. This is the aim of Thelema.

As I pointed out in the last chapter, true Thelemic magicians live their magick twenty-four hours a day. I have already described some exercises that will help you increase your daily awareness; now it's time to talk about the morality that goes with them.

Morality—there's another very unfashionable word—and with good reason. Practically every religion since the dawn of mankind has imposed a set of commandments on its adherents. Thelema has one commandment only: "Do what thou wilt shall be the whole of the Law." That's it. It's that simple.

You have only two choices in life: you can do what others think is right, or you can do what you think is right. If you choose the first way, then you should ask yourself why you think that someone else should know more about what is right for you than you do yourself—how can they get inside your skin and know what it feels like? If on the other hand you choose the second way, then you are a Thelemite.

Now you have probably one of two reactions here: either you nod sagely, and say "Of course, what other way could there be?" or your eyes open wide and you say "But—that could never work!" If you are of the first type, fine, you're a natural Thelemite, but you still have a lot of thinking to do. If you are of the second, I have to tell you that you are wrong; I know from my own experience and that of many of my friends that it works very well. Still, at least you are aware enough to see the difficulties inherent in such a seemingly simple proposition.

Let's examine this phrase: "Do what thou wilt shall be the whole of the Law." Notice that we do not say "Do whatever you like." We are talking here about your True Will. This is a concept that you have come across in earlier chapters. The word Thelema itself is Greek for Will. What is your True Will? It is your destiny, the Way through life which leads to the fulfillment of your Great Work. Each of us is individual and unique: as Liber AL puts it: "Every man and every woman is a star." Each of us has our own light to give to the world; each of us has our own orbit, our path through the universe, a way which is right for us, and us alone. Moral codes which spell out a set of rules for every person to follow identically simply lower each person's capacity for his or her own development.

By definition, to evolve is to become different from what has gone before. All things must change and grow, and a fixed moral code cannot grow with you. Only you can judge what action is right for you at any one time. To stop growing, to become rigid and unbending, is to start dying. As the ancient Chinese classic, the Dao De Jing puts it: "Rigidity and hardness are the stigmata of death; elasticity and adaptability of life." And as Thelemites we embrace Life in our arms, we live to the fullest manner we are capable, and we extend our capabilities as much as possible in order to be able to experience even more in the future. "Wisdom says: be strong! Then thou canst bear more rapture."—Liber AL.

Note that this idea of "Do what thou wilt" may be simple, but it is not *easy*. Fixed moral codes have one "advantage" in that in any given situation believers always know precisely what they are supposed to do and not do. Thelemites do not have this crutch to lean on. We must decide for ourselves what we must do, and it is this that is one of the greatest stumbling blocks for many who attempt this way. Thelemites cannot take the lazy way of simply following God's orders. We are gods, we *make* the orders for ourselves to follow. This can be very hard work, but ultimately it is much more fulfilling than just accepting the teachings of another. As Robert Anton Wilson says: "Convictions cause convicts," and Thelemites want to breathe the air of liberty; we are masters of our own fate.

For many people the Thelemic way is too hard at first, as they do not want to accept the responsibility of looking after themselves without a "big daddy" in heaven to tell them what to do. Remember that normally you cannot persuade them to

change, nor should you, for perhaps this way is their Will—
if they grow to accept our way in their own time, we should
rejoice, but we must not interfere too much. You can inform
people of Thelemic principles if they wish to know of them
(that's what this book is about after all), but you must never
try to force them into doing what you think is right. The line
between teaching and preaching is a fine one—be careful that
you don't step over it! If in doubt, keep silent, and respect the
beliefs of others, even when you disagree with them. Just
make sure that they respect your beliefs too!

This question of mutual respect is one reason why Crowley always advised aspirants to greet others in letters and conversations with the salutation "Do what thou wilt shall be the
whole of the Law." By beginning like this you are establishing the ground rules for the coming interaction. You are stating that you will respect the other person's point of view and
that you expect them to respect your point of view also. Of
course, starting conversations like this will get you some
funny looks! Mind you, people do have a surprising capacity
for tolerating what they will consider to be an amusing eccen-
tricity. Many Thelemites abbreviate this greeting to the simple
"93," a reference to the numerical value of the word Thelema
in Hebrew. Personally, I sometimes think that this just sounds
silly, though I am sure that the majority of Thelemites disagree with me. One advantage to saying "93" is that people
often ask what it means, which can lead to really interesting
conversations with total strangers.

Perhaps I should now confess that for years I did not use
any form of Thelemic greeting, mainly because I did not want
to force my own beliefs down someone else's throat. However, while writing this book, I thought I'd better check it out
before passing judgment, and I must say the result was a
pleasant surprise. It is a really good exercise in "everyday"
magick (see last chapter), and it's a great way of irritating
some of the assholes you meet.

Now the obvious criticism of the doctrine of the True
Will is the classic: "But if everyone just does what they want,

what's to stop someone raping me/shooting me/stopping me from watching television, etc." This is a very short-sighted view, based on the typical Old Aeon morality of the monotheistic slave religions like Christianity. These religions teach that humans are intrinsically evil, that we are all horrible monsters inside, only holding back our nasty impulses thanks to the guidelines that God has kindly given to us. Thelemites have no concept of "Original Sin"; we do not believe that people are basically Satanic glove-puppets. Rather the Thelemite realizes that each person is a pure and perfect star, each an essential part of the universe. We know that when we do our Wills, we have no desire to hurt others indiscriminately, for to do so is to destroy part of our universe, to reduce the complexity and wonderment of our lives. Each star is beautiful, and we are concerned with maximizing the beauty of life, not reducing it.

Note also that when I greet you with "Do what thou wilt," I am not only affirming my right to do *my* Will, but your right to do *yours*. It's "Do what *thou* wilt" that is to be our law, not "Do what *I* Will!"

When you have an impulse to interfere with the way that others live their lives, you are not allowing them the liberty to follow their True Wills, and you must remember "the Law is for All." All people have the right to do their Wills, so True Wills should never come into conflict with each other. If conflict does arise, you should examine yourself closely, for at least one person is not doing their True Will. In a non-Thelemic society this person will probably not be you, but if the fight is between Thelemites, then you may well be at fault. Conflict in this case can be a very useful thing, for it can be a pointer toward possible problems in your own development.

Liber AL states that "Love is the law, love under will." This shows that the nature of our True Wills must always be Love. Love is the yearning for things which are apart to become unified. Love is how we reach out beyond ourselves to that which we desire. Although we are individual stars, we must never make the mistake of assuming that we are alone within ourselves; we must not shut ourselves up in ivory towers of self-absorption. We shine with our innermost light, it is true, but the universe is full of other stars too, each shedding many-hued radiance towards us. Through Love we perceive many more possibilities than we already have, through Love we gain some understanding of the magnitude of this enormous cosmos we inhabit.

Note that Love must be under Will, however. Love is a function of the True Will, and our Love should never be used as a weapon or tool to manipulate the Will of others—nor should we allow others to restrict our Will, no matter how dearly we love them. Thelemic loving relationships are a great deal different from the norm. Emotional game-playing, one-upmanship, jealousy, all these things spring from lack of respect for the Will of others and should be absent. Honesty, trust, shared feelings, and freedom should characterize the Thelemic partnership. This is not easy, I know (I speak from experience), and can take great effort to achieve. But at least it never gets boring!

You can see now that this simple formula of "Do what thou wilt" has huge ramifications to the way that you approach your life. It is a charter for universal liberty, but it is not easy to put into practice. We live in a sick society, a society whose rules and laws are frequently contrary to Thelemic belief. Even our own minds can rebel against us when we try to put Thelemic ideals into practice. We have been educated away from our natural, instinctive godhood, and the repressions which have been sinking into our minds from an early age have twisted our consciousness, making it hard to accept our True Wills fully—and often making it even harder to accept the True Wills of others. You must endeavor to examine your actions and reactions carefully; try to see if what you are doing each moment is really what you Will to do. You must be very honest with others, but more than that, honest with yourself. The human mind has an almost infinite capacity for self-delusion, so watch out for this! The exercises that I have given in the previous chapters will help you develop a better understanding of yourself. Use them.

In order to make it easier to understand some of the ideas implicit in Thelema, Aleister Crowley wrote Liber OZ (see page 70). Although still simple and easy to understand, Liber OZ develops the concepts in a little more detail.

If you have gotten this far in the book, you should have no objections to anything expressed in Liber OZ, except perhaps to section 5: "Man has the right to kill those who thwart these rights." Most people who read this for the first time are deeply shocked—I myself was no exception. But after thinking the whole thing through, I began to realize that this was an essential part of the system too, for without the capacity to defend our rights, we have no real liberty. It is all very well to preach "love your enemy" (and I believe we should love our enemies), but when some asshole comes along to stick you in a concentration camp, simply following his orders is not going to help you achieve your True Will (unless following orders is your True Will—somehow, in this case, I doubt it). Our enemies must be aware that we follow our True Wills, come what may, and that we will fight to defend our right to live in our own way. We mean no harm to others who respect our rights—we encourage them to free themselves also—but we will not bow down to any man or woman. Life is the most precious gift we possess, but if someone thwarts our rights, they take away our life, for eating, thinking, loving—these things are our lives. And if my enemy feels that human life is unimportant, he condemns himself, for he is human too.

Thelema is not a peaceful religion—but then again how many peaceful Christians do you know? At least we are not hypocritical about our beliefs. We state what we think; we do not try to hide from the truth. Christians say "Thou shalt not kill," but they have the bloodthirstiest history of any religion.

If you still feel uncomfortable about all this, remember that all that Liber OZ says is that you have the *right* to kill those who would thwart your rights—just because you have

Liber LXXVII

Oz:

"the law of
the strong:
this is our law
and the joy
of the world."
— *AL. II. 21*

"Do what thou wilt shall be the whole of the Law."
— *AL. I. 40*

"thou has no right but to do thy will. Do that, and no
other shall say nay." — *AL. I. 42–3*

"Every man and every woman is a star." — *AL. I. 3*

There is no god but man.

1. Man has the right to live by his own law —
   to live in the way that he wills to do:
   to work as he will:
   to play as he will:
   to rest as he will:
   to die when and how he will.

2. Man has the right to eat what he will:
   to drink what he will:
   to dwell where he will:
   to move as he will on the face of the earth.

3. Man has the right to think what he will:
   to speak what he will:
   to write what he will:
   to draw, paint, carve, etch, mould, build as he will:
   to dress as he will.

4. Man has the right to love as he will: —
   "take your fill and will of love as ye will,
   when, where and with whom ye will." — *AL. I. 51*

5. Man has the right to kill those who would thwart
   these rights.

"the slaves shall serve." — *AL. II. 58*

"Love is the law, love under will." — *AL. I. 57*

Aleister Crowley

that right does not mean that you *have* to exercise it. There is no Thelemic law that states that you have to go out and blast everyone in sight with a .44 Magnum (please don't!)—do not forget that the biggest enemy standing in the way of your True Will is usually your own ego.

The phrase below section 5 in Liber OZ, "the slaves shall serve," is also often the cause of some confusion. It does *not* mean that we should enslave other people—quite the opposite in fact ("the Law is for All," remember). The phrase does not say that some people should be slaves for us—it implies that the slaves shall become servants. Slaves are those who are forced to do something against their Will; servants are those who voluntarily assist others and are rewarded for doing so. If it is someone's Will to serve, then by all means they can do so—but they should never be *forced* into serving others. Even if they wish to be slaves, we cannot enslave them—they serve through their own choice. Be wary of making the mistake of assuming that those who wish to serve are somehow inferior. The person who paints the house is in no wise inferior to the person who owns the house. If they are performing their True Will, who are you to criticize them? Better for you to concentrate on doing your own Will, rather than interfering in the Will of others. And if it is your Will to serve others—do it! ". . . thou hast no right but to do thy will. Do that, and no other shall say nay."

Read this phrase in Liber OZ again, carefully. There is an important lesson here. Never allow yourself to take any phrase at face value in the world of magick. Think about its content and meaning carefully. This is doubly important when you are reading Liber AL or one of the other Thelemic Holy Books, which frequently have hidden messages buried within seemingly innocuous sentences.

I have gone into the subject of the True Will in some depth here and have been treating it very seriously, but when all's said and done, the great thing about being a Thelemite is that it's fun! "Do what thou Wilt" *does* mean that you can go out and do all those things you always wanted to do, and you won't spend eternity burning in hell as a punishment for your sins. To the Thelemite "The word of Sin is Restriction." You sin against yourself when you hold back from fulfilling your Will—so don't hold back any longer. As psychology teaches us, repression of natural instincts is the major cause of neurosis, and the most natural instinct of all is to have a good time. As a friend of mine once put it: "At the end of the day, it's all just sex and drugs and rock 'n' roll, isn't it?" I had to agree that he had summed it up pretty succinctly.

To the Thelemite, the sexual impulse is practically a sacred thing in itself. Our sexuality is the most fundamental expression of our Will: we have no taboos or mores restricting sexual activity. Any sexual act between mutually consenting adults is a wonderful thing—in fact it is a holy thing, for it is the living embodiment of our Love under Will.

Drugs are a subject a little more tricky to deal with. Liber AL says: "To worship me take wine & strange drugs whereof I will tell my prophet, & be drunk thereof! They shall not harm ye at all," which is pretty clear. Or is it? Notice that this only applies to *worship*, not to taking drugs for social purposes. Also notice the phrase "strange drugs." The drugs we take must be strange; in their strangeness lie new experiences. But once we have assimilated these new sensations, the drugs are no longer strange to us. We must be especially wary of becoming addicted to drugs, for to the addict the drug has become an intrinsic part of existence—it is not at all strange any more, and we have only been promised that *strange* drugs cannot harm us. The addict who is using drugs that are no longer strange has no such safeguard. Be careful, people! By all means experiment, but do not let your Will be taken from you.

As for the rock 'n' roll, that's another story.

FURTHER STUDY

Magick—Part I, Chapter 3: Yama and Niyama
Magick Without Tears—Chapter 15: Sex Morality
Magick Without Tears—Chapter 31: Religion: Is Thelema a "New Religion?"
Magick Without Tears—Chapter 78: Sore Spots

CHAPTER SEVEN

CONDITIONING AND CONCENTRATION

In our preceding yoga sections the exercises given were concerned first with stilling the body (through asana and pranayama), then with stilling the mind (through mantra). You will have already noticed by now that these things are not at all separate, for when you affect one, you automatically affect the other. The mind and body are tightly connected by an interface so subtle, yet so strong, that I could easily fill an entire book on this subject alone (if I understood it, which even after years of study, I don't). You are no doubt aware of the power of your autonomic nervous system, which is capable of pulling your hand away from a fire even before your brain has even begun to recognize that it is hot. Yet not only do you have no control over this part of your system, you are incapable of even communicating with it, except in emergencies. How do you expect to be able to control and manipulate the higher energies of your psyche if you cannot even control the most basic part of your mind-body interface?

Do you have any control over fear? Over your sexual responses? Over hunger? You probably think you have, but what you call control is largely just the capability to push your desires to one side of your consciousness and try to forget about them, which is *not* control.

"Why do I need this control?" I hear you cry. The reason is the same reason that we began this book with yoga exercises: because as long as you remain the slave of distraction, you cannot even hope to find out your True Will, much less perform it. Your body is the chariot of your spirit and the mind the horses that pull it. As magicians we do not travel the smooth featureless highway of the common man, but the unexplored mountain paths that lead us to the peaks of human experience. The chariot must be strong enough to cope with the bumpy ride ahead, and the horses must be kept on a tight rein, firmly directed by our Will. The yoke that keeps the horses together and connects them to the chariot is the link that our entire journey depends on; if that link is weak, we will find ourselves dumped unceremoniously on our backsides just at the moment we are starting to pick up some speed. Our chariot yoke is yoga. Thus far on our travels in the Land of OZ we have merely been skirting the foothills of magick. Before we launch an assault on the summit, it is time to do a little bodywork (and finally terminate this overly extended metaphor).

In our work, our bodies and minds will become subjected to a great deal of stress on occasion. So how to tell what is too much stress? The problem with stress is that when it is at its worst is usually the time when your mind is so preoccupied that you have little capacity left to observe it and deal with it. The thing to do now is to learn just how far you can go in a given direction before you run into severe problems—to find out your tolerance limits. To this end you should now sit down and work out the limitations of your body. Make a list of things that you should check out. For example, how long you can hold your breath; how long you can go without food or drink; how long you can go without sleep; how long you can go without speaking; how far you can run before you fall down; how long you can continue sex without orgasm, etc. With a little thought I'm sure you can come up with some more examples. Then work out a program for testing all these things. Holding your breath is easy. Just sit down with a stopwatch and check it. It shouldn't take longer than a couple of minutes, unless you are a mutant.

Make a note of this in your Magical Diary, then decide which thing you will check out next—not speaking perhaps. Decide on a time to shut your mouth, then see how long you can go on without opening it again (I found this one especially hard!). Remember that even wordless cries count as speaking, so perhaps your sexual activities may also be affected by this.

Be aware that as you do these exercises you are putting your body under considerable stress, so after you have finished each one allow yourself some time to recover your natural state; otherwise you will be adversely affecting the results of the next test. And of course you should certainly not run two of these tests at the same time. Always take careful notes of your feelings about the exercise before, during, and after its performance. Try to combine scientific objectiveness with personal feeling—it is possible, and definitely desirable, to have both.

I highly recommend that as part of this set of exercises you try various forms of sensory deprivation. I first had the inspiration for this when I became friendly with a blind man. On visiting him for the first time, I was amazed at how many everyday things had become difficult for him since he had lost his sight—all his socks were white for example, since he had no way of telling otherwise if they matched or not and he didn't want to look silly in front of his sighted friends by appearing dressed in odd socks. If this seems a rather petty example to you, then you have a 100 percent need of sensory deprivation exercises. First exercise: blindfold yourself—and I do mean blind! For this you need a very strong piece of thick black material. Fold it in such a way that you can tie it tightly around your forehead—not around your eyes. When the knot is tight and you are sure it won't slip, pull the band down to cover your eyes. It should be very tight and probably quite uncomfortable at first; don't worry about this, it will stretch after a while. The band should be thick enough to ensure that no light whatsoever gets to your eyes—you must be in complete darkness. You will stay this way for at least twenty-four hours, including when you are asleep (waking up blind is an interesting experience). I would advise that you arrange to have someone around most of the time to keep an eye on you (ha ha), because being in a blind state can be dangerous as well as uncomfortable. Even something as simple as making a cup of tea becomes a very hazardous experience, so beware. You should also try going shopping and walking in the forest (with your companion to guide you, of course). Wear dark glasses and a hat to help disguise the bandage around your eyes, so that people don't automatically assume that there is something wrong with you. When you have done this exercise for a day or two, you will know more about sight than you ever thought possible. The sensation you get when you first take off the blindfold at the end of the exercise is quite astonishing.

You can easily adapt this exercise to the other senses—wear earplugs, encase your hands in plaster. Use your imagination to think of different variations. You are an intensely complicated creature; your body is a beautiful, wonderful, mysterious machine. Delve deep into its mysteries.

* * *

I have already pointed out how our bodies' reactions betray us when we stick our hands in a fire. Now this is an interesting function of our mind-body system. Can we not turn it around and use it to our advantage? If we could bring this automatic reaction system under our control, we would have a very valuable tool indeed. Remember that automatic reactions like this (controlled via the spinal cord) are generally much faster than those controlled by the normal route via the brain. And the more functions that are under automatic control, the more free processing time is left in our brains, processing time that can be used for other, more important things (like having fun ... oops, I mean for doing complicated magical work, of course).

When a dog (or a human for that matter) is presented with food, there is an automatic body function which increases the amount of saliva in the mouth in order to aid digestion. The Russian scientist Pavlov demonstrated that by ringing a bell while feeding a dog, he could condition the dog's responses in such a way that the dog would begin salivating every time he heard the bell, whether there was food present or not. The next exercise takes this basic idea and applies it to magical work.

This exercise is a variation of another Crowley work

called Liber Jugorum. Using it will make you aware of previously hidden powers in yourself and simultaneously strengthen those powers. First, I want you to pick a simple bodily act, crossing your legs for example or lifting your arm above the level of your head or clenching your left fist. Anything that you do not do very frequently will suffice. Now you will swear an oath:

From this moment on, for the space of one week, I will endeavor not to [insert your chosen action here].

Easy, huh? You will have no problems at all sticking to your oath, I know. Now, just to make it a little more interesting, we will add a little punishment for you should the impossible happen and you accidentally perform the forbidden action. You will carry around on your person at all times a very sharp pin. Any time you do what you have sworn to try not to do, you will take this pin in your right hand and you will jab it very sharply into the back of your left hand (reverse these directions if you're left-handed). And make sure that it hurts too.

After a couple of days you will have a hand that resembles a very old dartboard. If you begin to lose the sensation in your left hand through too much jabbing (and it can easily happen, believe me), switch hands or move to your legs. I don't recommend using your face—you are too beautiful for that. At all times you must carry a pin with you; a good way to ensure that you always have one handy is to wear a metal badge on your jacket or shirt and use the pin on that. It is *vital* that you jab yourself every single time you perform the forbidden act, so monitor your actions very carefully during the week. Each day, make a detailed note in your Magical Diary of how many times you performed the unmentionable deed. At the end of the week, breathe a huge sigh of relief. Now pick another different physical action for next week's practice, and start the whole process again. If you like, I will allow you to take a day or two off in between.

After a couple of weeks of this, you should find that your body is acting very differently than before. Every time that you unconsciously begin to do what you are not supposed to do, your body will try to stop itself automatically. It is a very peculiar sensation indeed to see your arm suddenly halt in midair, then a split second later realize why you just did it.

When you have become reasonably proficient in this exercise (after about a month or two, perhaps), vary it a little. For the next month, instead of making a physical action forbidden, you will pick a word that is forbidden. This should be some small simple word, such as "the" or "and." As you can probably imagine, this is much harder than before, but not impossible. After a few of weeks of this, go for the big one. For a week, refuse to say the word "I" or any word referring to the first person, e.g., my, mine, etc. When you need to refer to yourself, you can use a substitute, such as referring to yourself in the third person, e.g., "This person thinks" instead of "I think." Doing this will really change the way you see yourself; this person guarantees it.

If you feel really confident after all of this, you can push the exercise even further, by forbidding a certain *thought* to arise. This really is hard, so get some new extra sharp pins (the old ones should be fairly dull by this time).

If you think this exercise seems too painful, you are far too squeamish about hurting yourself and thus have even more reason to do it. Bear in mind that the method I have described is a lot less painful than the method Crowley gives. He advises that you slash your forearm with a cut-throat razor every time you perform the forbidden act. I've seen photographs of an aspirant who did this, and it's not a pretty sight. There is no doubt that using a razor is very, very effective, so if you're really dedicated, go for it. I don't advise it though. The most important point to remember is that you must cause sudden sharp pain, because the pain system in your body is the path along which you send the conditioning messages. The advantage of the pin method (apart from its convenience) is that the pain caused is very strong, but only lasts for a brief moment. A few seconds later you will hardly feel it, but it will have done its job by then. Another variation on this is to wear a rubber band around your wrist, and when you perform the forbidden act, simply pull the band away from your wrist and let it snap back sharply. Same principle, equally painful (if done properly)!

I adopted this pin method, rather than using a razor, because when I first worked this exercise myself, I was still at school, and sitting in class chopping bits out of my arm with a sharp blade would have probably resulted in a forced trip to see a psychiatrist. Using a pin was a way of making the exercise unobtrusive, but kept it effective, for it is a twenty-four hour exercise, and must be done all the time, during work periods, while watching TV, whatever. Remember, it applies during sex as well—it can make it even more interesting actually ...

One important point to remember when performing the preceding exercise is that the pain you cause yourself is not in any way a punishment for your own failure or wrongdoing. We are usually brought up to believe in the concept that we are rewarded for doing right, punished for doing wrong, so there is a tendency in the minds of many people to see this exercise from such a perspective. Nothing could be further from the truth. The main confusion arises from a basic misunderstanding of the function of pain. When you are hurt, you feel pain. You don't feel pain because God is trying to punish you for hurting yourself; you feel pain purely and simply because pain is the method by which your body tells your brain that something urgently requires its care and attention. Pain is not "bad" or "evil," although of course it is also not designed to be pleasant. It certainly has nothing at all to do with punishment—although human beings sometimes use it for such a purpose, in the same way that they sometimes use it for a sexual purpose. Pain is like the ringing of the telephone—it is not a very pleasing noise; it is loud and raucous so that it attracts our attention away from the other things that we are doing. In itself it means nothing, but it signals that an event is occurring that may be important to us, whether good or bad.

In the Liber Jugorum exercise, by causing pain to be associated with a conscious activity, you learn to affect your psyche from two opposite directions at once. You train your autonomic nervous system to respond in a more conscious manner, and in doing so, your consciousness learns more about the linkages throughout your entire structure. Both parts of you, normally so far distant from each other, reach out to become more closely connected.

In connection with this, it should be noted that Liber Jugorum is thus not connected with what psychologists call "negative reinforcement." There is nothing at all negative (or positive) about the exercise. These ideas that any behavior can be somehow intrinsically positive or negative are, to my mind, nonsensical. The point of the exercise is not to train yourself to avoid doing "a bad thing," but to learn the mechanisms by which you function, so that you will then be capable of understanding yourself more fully, and thus be able to change your own behavior patterns whenever and however you desire.

* * *

Another exercise associated to this one is the adoption of different personalities. This has been exhaustively explored in Luke Rhinehart's book *The Diceman,* which I thoroughly recommend. We are accustomed to think of our personalities as being our Selves. This is totally false. The word "personality" springs from the Latin word "persona," meaning a mask—in ancient drama the characters are differentiated only by the masks they wear; in the modern world it is not greatly different. Your personality is only the clothing you wear over your soul. In Thelemic terms, we call the soul, or starry nature, by the Egyptian word "Khabs," and the personality by the name "Khu" (as in Ra-Hoor-KHU-it, meaning roughly: the magical personality of the Sun). Liber AL says:

> The Khabs is in the Khu, not the Khu in the Khabs.
> Worship then the Khabs, and behold my light shed over you!

We must stop identifying ourselves as our personalities. Instead we must worship the Khabs; we must explore our true nature that lies below the level of the personality. We do this by first understanding what a fragile, artificial thing our personality really is.

Here are some things you can try. Pick two different personalities. For example, one person who believes in democracy, Christianity, loves family and eating meat. The other person is a Communist atheist who dislikes family and is vegetarian. When you wake up in the morning, the first thing you do is toss a coin. If it comes up heads, for the rest of the day you are person number one, and all you do and say during the whole day must reflect your new personality. If the coin comes up tails, you are person number two, and the same strictures apply. You can also apply the pin treatment here if you want to make it even more fun. You can change the two basic personalities after a few days or extend the choice. I'd suggest six different sets of beliefs, chosen by rolling a six-sided die each morning.

Probably the best way of adopting different personalities, and certainly the most fun, is fantasy role-playing games, such as Dungeons & Dragons. In these games you can learn to create entire, full-blown, living and breathing, new personalities, which are also essentially you. The big advantage here is that it is not a solo pursuit, but a social one, and the feedback created by the interaction with the other players allows one to identify deeply with the new personality very easily. A must for the contemporary magician in my view.

A few years ago I underwent a very interesting personality change exercise. It was prompted by a chance remark made by my then girlfriend. We were walking past a building site when my girlfriend, who was a divinely sexy creature, was spotted by several primitive males, who immediately responded to her presence in the time-honored fashion of wolf-whistling and shouting remarks of an overtly sexual nature. This really annoyed her, as you might imagine. I told her to ignore it, it was a waste of energy for her to get annoyed about something so insignificant. She replied that it was all very well for me to say that, but that I wasn't a woman and so could not understand how horrible it was. This got me thinking. At the time I was running a business selling second-hand women's clothing from the fifties and sixties, and by chance the very next day a pair of very large high heeled shoes arrived in the shop. I am physically quite slim and short, so there was no problem getting other women's clothes to fit me. The next evening, before going to a party, I spent a considerable amount of time applying makeup to my face and back-combing my (long) hair. A fur wrap to cover the Adam's apple and gloves to cover the hands—the two most obvious giveaways—and as long as I didn't speak I was a woman, and a very good-looking woman too, much to my own surprise.

Walking to the party in high heels was ... er ... interesting, but I soon had the correct hip-swinging action. At the party about 50 percent of the guests knew me, and I had the fascinating experience of seeing my friends' basic sexual responses turned upside down. The boys either freaked out totally and became very aggressive, or freaked out totally and tried to hide it very unsuccessfully. The girls loved it, thinking either that it was really cute, or alternatively thinking that it was an incredible turn-on. Everybody, and I mean *everybody*, treated me completely differently than they had before, whether they knew that I was a man or not. For the first time in my life I felt that I actually realized something about the primal sexuality that flows through us all the time. For the next six months or so, I divided my time by randomly switching between appearing as a man or as a woman; occasionally just to complicate things further, I would use very masculine expressions while dressed as a woman, or vice versa.

I would point out that I did not consider myself to be a transvestite—I got no intrinsic sexual thrill out of wearing women's clothing, although it had a pronounced positive effect on my girlfriend, which was wonderful. I was more interested in observing the reactions of those around me and in observing my own attitudes toward gender roles, and how they changed. To be honest, from the beginning I found the concept of a item of clothing being intrinsically either masculine or feminine to be faintly ludicrous.

I have not described this part of my magical career in order to advise all readers to change their mode of sexual expression—your sexuality is your own, it is not my place to comment upon it. But I want you to realize just how deep your personality penetrates and how far you can go in order to learn about yourself and others around you. Examine everything!

These personality changing exercises are, to my mind, absolutely necessary for all magicians, for as you gain magical power in your studies, so you will be tempted to expand your ego at the expense of your True Will. Your Will springs directly from your Khabs, your soul, not from the level of the ego, and the exercises above will make that very clear to you. This does not mean to say that there is something intrinsically evil or wrong about your ego—far from it. Nevertheless, the ego is not the seat of your consciousness; it is just another part of the multifaceted jewel that is your mind. It must be understood and trained, like every other part of your mind and body. The ego is a good servant but a bad master.

* * *

Thus far we have been attempting to train the more unconscious parts of the mind. Now we turn our attention in the opposite direction, to the powers of mental concentration.

Whereas the practices described above are primarily designed to teach you how to stop from doing or thinking a certain thing, the next exercises are about learning to concentrate on a certain thing to the exclusion of all else. The yoga term for this is Dharana.

This is, in essence, the simplest exercise of all. All you basically have to do is fix the picture of an object in your mind and concentrate on that and on nothing else. You can pick any object, but to begin with the best is some form of elementary two-dimensional geometrical shape, such as a square or a triangle. Although this exercise is simple, it's not easy—on the contrary it's probably the hardest in the book (there's a lesson here...). Keep the figure as basic as possible, without color to start with, just a monochrome line drawing will do. It will help to draw this figure on a card before you begin, then sit in your asana for a while staring at the picture. Now close your eyes and visualize the figure floating before you. Try to keep it absolutely steady and firm, and do not allow it to waver or fade away. Do not allow any other thoughts to intrude. You will find this to be exceedingly difficult I think, so don't try for too long at one sitting; even a minute or two is enough. Keep careful note in your Diary of how many times your thoughts broke away from your control.

After a few attempts with line drawings, you can move to colored shapes. The group of elemental symbols known as tattwas are ideal for this. The tattwas consist of: a yellow square (Earth), a light blue circle (Air), a silver crescent (Water), a red equilateral triangle (Fire), and a black or dark blue egg-shape (Spirit). Each of these symbols should be painted on a card with either a black or a white background. With these tattwa figures you may find that you occasionally have a tendency to drift off into a bit of a dream world during your concentration. Although this is a very normal occurrence and can be very interesting, it is not what we want at the moment, so try to resist the temptation to dream as much as possible. At this stage it is important that you concentrate—you will get your fill of dreaming later, when the time comes.

As your concentration improves, you can expand on this exercise in innumerable ways. Try concentrating on other senses, touch, taste, smell, and hearing (this last is the absolute hardest). Instead of two-dimensional figures, you can try three-dimensional figures. Four-dimensional figures are possible, but I don't recommend it—it is a recipe for severe brain-ache. Try moving 3-D figures: Crowley suggests pistons, which is quite a good idea, and human beings that you know well. Figures can be combined with the smells, sounds, etc. All of this should definitely NOT be attempted until you have had reasonable experience with the simpler forms. As in all the exercises I explain to you, remember to get the basics right first, before you move on.

When your concentration practice has become very good indeed—and this can take months, if not years—sooner or later a very curious thing will happen. One day you will be concentrating hard on your chosen figure, when suddenly you will achieve total concentration. At that moment the entire relationship between you and the figure will change utterly. You will become completely identified with the sign; it will no longer be perceived as in any way separate from your consciousness. This is the state called Dharana in yoga. Not only will this signal a change in your concentration practice, from this moment on your whole perception of the universe is forever changed, for you will have transcended the duality of existence for probably the first time in your life.

It is virtually impossible to describe this process in any greater detail, since the language we use is itself based on a dualistic structure. However, this state of Dharana is so unmistakable that there is no need for me to explain it further. There is no specific exercise that can be used to achieve this state; pure concentration is the way. Do not attempt to force it either, because by doing so you will likely end up in an illusory dream state that you *think* is Dharana but most likely isn't. The best bet is to attempt to resist the onset of

Dharana as much as possible, for seeking after it will only hinder your concentration—and Dharana can only occur when concentration is total.

I realize that by now I have given you a very great deal of difficult and frequently boring and repetitive exercises to do. I know it's hard (I've done them all myself, remember ...), but as a great teacher once told me: "When I talk about the Great Work, I do mean *work*!" Hang in there, never forget that all this time you are changing, evolving, growing toward recognition of your own Godhood. If you are getting a little downhearted, try reading back through your Diary from the beginning and see how much your reactions have changed since you started working with this book. Don't worry if your thoughts are sometimes confused—that's natural. You are exploring the labyrinths of your own mind, and the starways of the cosmos. If occasionally you have become a little lost, it's no big problem, for "Ra-Hoor abideth at the helm," and in the end the Thelemic current will carry the ship of your spirit faithfully to the shores of the Great Sea of Nuit.

FURTHER STUDY

Magick—Part I, Chapters 4, 5, 6, 7
Magick—Appendix VII: Liber E vel Exercitiorum, Part V
Magick—Appendix VII: Liber III vel Jugorum

CHAPTER EIGHT

INVOCATION

Until this chapter we have been dealing with the fundamental training exercises of magick. You have had your mind and body pushed, pulled, and pummeled, until now it should be honed into a nearly perfect instrument of your Will. From this point on we will stretch it even further, beyond your normal consciousness. Instead of just dealing with your own innate powers, you will be dealing with those giant storehouses of cosmic energies which we call gods.

Of course, we have encountered gods before—in the pentagram ritual, in the Assumption of the God-form of Hoor-paar-kraat, and in Liber Resh. When the fundamental ideas of these three exercises are combined, they form the basis of the major work of the magician: the invocation.

What is an invocation? The word springs from the Latin "invocare" meaning to call in. When you invoke, you not only call the gods into your presence and talk with them, you call the gods inside your very self. You literally become the god you invoke.

Many of us who have been brought up in Western European influenced cultures have a great deal of trouble with this simple point. I have seen magicians of many years' experience who had great difficulty even comprehending its full implications. If you have been performing the Nu-Sphere ritual regularly (and you should have been by now), this idea of invocation should be almost second nature to you. Think back to the text. You state that your god is above, below, to the right, and to the left of you; then you affirm that your god is within you. When you have surrounded yourself on all sides by the god, you can then call the god to dwell inside your soul. Once you have done this, you go one step further—you become god fully and completely. You shout "There is no God where I am!" because you yourself have attained full identification with that god; you *are* that god, you are a totally unique and indivisible force of the cosmos. Study this process carefully, for herein lies the key to invocation.

While performing the rituals given in earlier chapters, you may well have noticed that sometimes they go better than other times. This normally depends on what sort of mood you are in, what sort of day you have had, what time you performed the work, what the weather was like, etc. In other words, the efficacy of an invocation is very much dependent on the mood of the magician, which in turn is very dependent on the environmental conditions prevailing at that moment. So in order to maximize the effects of our rituals, we must ensure that the environment for the ritual is as closely fitted to the ritual as possible.

Let's consider the environment—of what does it consist? Well, basically it consists of everything that the magician can sense—all sights, sounds, smells, emotions, whatever. The place where you are working, the clothes you are wearing, the things you are using, all contribute strongly to the way that you approach the ritual. So before we even begin to launch our first big invocation, we must prepare our environment, our Temple of Art.

You already have a temple, in a sense, for by now you should have a place which you normally use for your magick—perhaps your bedroom, or a spare room in your house, or whatever. You know which quarter is East; perhaps you have a Stele of Revealing set up there. The first thing you will add is an altar.

The altar is a symbol of your basis of your Work; it is what your Work rests on. You have already noticed that much of practical magick depends on the number four—we have four quarters to the circle, we do our breathing in a 4 x 4 rhythm, etc. Four is the number of the material elements: Earth, Air, Water, and Fire, and we will try to keep this fourfold elemental attribution as much as possible. Thus our altar will be square, preferably cubical. Traditionally the altar should be composed of a double cube, i.e., two cubes set one on top of the other; and this is indeed an excellent arrangement. At the moment, I myself use just a single black cube, since it fits well in my apartment. Another possibility is the use of a small cupboard which has the advantage that you can keep your other bits of magical equipment inside. Your altar may be plain in color or have a design on top. Personally I prefer to keep it plain and then cover it with a cloth. This covering may be of any material you desire, though silk is perhaps best, and should be of an appropriate color and design. A common and very effective design is black silk with a large gold or silver pentagram applied. One magical group of my acquaintance uses a European flag (deep blue background with a circle of twelve gold stars—the Zodiac), which looks excellent and symbolizes Nuit perfectly—and which is certainly not difficult to obtain if you live in Europe.

You already know from the work you have done with the pentagram ritual that magical rituals are normally done within a circular area, so the next thing to construct is a magick circle. Of course, you always construct an imaginary astral circle when you perform a pentagram rite, but it is always helpful to have a material basis for your work as well. Your magick circle can be very simple or very complicated, or any point in between. The first things to think about in this case are the practical things—what the size of the circle should be and where you can put it. This depends mainly on what the conditions in your temple are. As regards size, the traditional circle should be nine feet (three meters) in diameter, but this is normally a bit too big for those of you who live in bedsits. In this case, I'd say just figure out how much space you've got and take the maximum size circle that will fit in comfortably, bearing in mind that you do need to leave a few centimeters around the outside of your circle as well so don't go right up to the wall. If you are really stuck for space, don't worry too much, but do what you can to get the most space possible. I've worked in circles that were barely big enough to sit down in, and it was all right, if a touch difficult when it came to drawing pentagrams.

You can construct the circle in several different ways. The most obvious way is to paint it on the floor, although for many of us that may not be a viable solution. If you don't have a nosy landlord who might object and you don't mind disfiguring your floor, then by all means do it this way. If, however, you are sixteen years old and live with your parents, I certainly do not advise bringing a couple of pots of paint up the stairs and slapping it around when your mother is out shopping.

If you don't want to leave paint on the floor, you could try drawing a circle using chalk that does not make a permanent impression. In my experience this is not a fantastic idea, as the chalk can sometimes be more permanent than you bargained for, and you can end up spending a couple of exciting hours with a scrubbing brush and a bucket.

If you are able to paint your floor, but don't want casual visitors to be aware of it, it is easy (and quite common among occultists) to paint the floor and cover it with a carpet during everyday life. This is what I did a few years ago in a previous house. On moving to another place, however, this option was not open to me, so I started thinking laterally and came up with the solution of painting the circle upon the carpet itself and rolling up the carpet when I wasn't performing magick. Yes, I know this might sound obvious now, but it wasn't so obvious at the time. This is really an ideal answer to the problem, and I thoroughly recommend it. Simply get hold of a carpet or rug, preferably plain in color, that you can paint on without too much difficulty (not shag-pile!). I used an old grey-brown military blanket, which was soft and warm, but strong and nicely neutral in color, and it has served me well for many years now. The best colors to go for are probably earthy brown or black for the base color of the carpet with green for the outline color of the circle itself and red for the details that you will add later. These are only suggestions, at the end of the day I think you can use your own judgment as to what you will feel comfortable with.

The other big advantage in using a rug or blanket like

this is that it comes in very handy for yoga practice, and it is really very nice to have a firm warm blanket to sit on, coupled with a magick circle surrounding you while you meditate.

If you have problems even with using a carpet, the easiest solution of all is to use a long length of cord, and just lay it on the floor in a (roughly) circular shape. This has the advantage of being cheap and easy, and very portable—and doesn't leave potentially embarrassing stains on the floor. The best to use is thick green cord, the sort that you often find used as a belt on a dressing gown—you can buy it in any large department store.

Until now I have been describing only a very basic circle, and although this is perfectly adequate, it can be good to make your circle a little more interesting. The traditional magick circle is actually composed of two circles, one inside the other, with the space that is formed between them used for the writing of divine names. These words act to strengthen the magical barrier which the circle symbolizes. You can use any names of any gods that you associate with power and protection—the names of the principal Thelemic gods, Nuit, Hadit, Ra-Hoor-Khuit and Hoor-paar-kraat might be a good choice (see page 94).

You may use as many or as few names as you wish, though bear in mind that too many will look a bit squashed together, whereas just one or two might look stretched. Four is good, as it divides the circle into the four elemental quarters. If you are using a cord circle, you can still use pieces of paper with the names written on them and placed around the inside of the ring.

Around the outside of the circle you should place candles—at least four of them is advised, but more or less any number is OK. Ensure that the candle holders are very stable and that the candles are fixed well in their holders. Make sure that there are no hanging drapes (or drooping altar cloths!) nearby. I have personally seen things get set on fire during rituals on several occasions, and when one's robe is alight, it does tend to disturb the calm, meditative ambiance some-

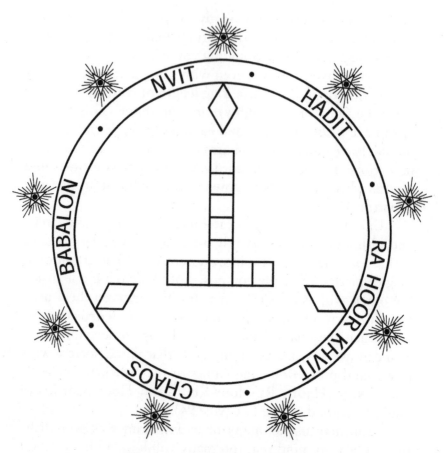

TRADITIONAL MAGICK CIRCLE

what, if you know what I mean. Small night lights are very safe, cheap, and practical though they do need proper holders as the metal bases they come in are not enough for real safety.

The candles around the outside of the circle act not only to provide illumination for you during your workings, but they also symbolize the light that you shed to the universe beyond. The circle represents your own universe, all that you are and that you control, but you should remember that outside your universe lies another in darkness and without understanding. Your magick not only transforms your world, but the energy you create for yourself and within yourself also spreads out to light the world around you, bringing warmth and comfort to those who have not yet discovered how they may see by their own inner light.

In order to bring out the inner light most efficiently, we need tools, and this brings us to the four main magical weapons: the disk, the sword, the cup, and the wand. Note that again we have the elemental number four. These weapons are rather badly named—tools or instruments might be a more appropriate terminology but traditionally they are known as weapons, so we'll stick to that for now.

The first weapon you will need is the disk, or pantacle. This is attributed to the element of Earth and should be a flat square or circle. The square shape is appropriate in keeping with the foursquare nature of Earthy things, but perhaps the circle is better in that it has more of an implication of activity, like a revolving wheel. The Earth may be the most "fixed" of the elements, but never make the mistake of thinking that anything, no matter how stable it seems, is unchanging. The Earth we walk on seems solid and unmoving, but is continually rushing around the Sun at an enormous velocity; it is just that we normally do not perceive it to be so (an important lesson here—always remember that ideas that may seem perfectly logical and natural to you may well be so only because of a defect in your own perception). The circle is also reminiscent of a coin, which is definitely a symbol of the material world. Your Earth pantacle can be of any size and substance that you prefer, but perhaps not too big for practical reasons. Traditionally wax is a favorite material to use, and this has the advantage of being easy to carve into; however, don't go holding it near hot candles! My advice is to go for a small flat metal disk of brass or copper, about ten centimeters in diameter.

On your disk you must now inscribe a figure which you will choose for yourself. The figure should be a design which symbolizes your understanding of the universe. This is not usually easy to work out in a few minutes, so you should allow yourself a few days (or maybe weeks) to meditate carefully on what design you can make which can symbolize the universe for you. Some magicians end up using extremely complicated patterns indeed, some end up with very simple designs. Neither is better than the other; you must decide for yourself how you see things around you. This process of choosing a figure which represents the universe is similar to the process of making mandalas, which is common in many cultures, most notably those of the Indian subcontinent, so I suggest that you check out a few of these mandalas during your studies—there are several useful books on the subject available.

Your design is probably best formed of combinations of simple geometrical figures—crosses are good, representing the four elements for example; the pentagram is always a good choice; perhaps a six-pointed star (hexagram) representing the union of material and spiritual. I have seen people use triangles, seven-pointed stars, signs of the zodiac, lots of things. When you have decided what you wish to use, you can paint it on your disk or engrave it. Painting is nice if you like color, but perhaps engraving is more permanent. Anyone can engrave given a little practice—I recommend that you purchase an electric engraving tool. These are not too expensive and are great fun. After a week with one of these, every piece of metal, glass, and ceramic in your house will have engravings on it!

Despite all my recommendations above, don't forget that the pantacle is, and must be, a very personal thing, and feel free to disagree with my suggestions if they feel wrong to you. For many years I myself have used a pantacle made from a large sheet of transparent Perspex, with a modified ancient Egyptian design painted on one side. This is highly untraditional and has surprised many of my magician friends when they've seen it, but what the hell, I like it, and the symbolism fits, and that's what counts.

The finding of a pantacle design is itself an excellent magical exercise which helps you to draw all your knowledge, experience, and desires into one unity, and at the end of the day, that is the function of the magical disk. It contains the entire basis of your work in one small instrument; it is the stability in your work. When you hold your disk in your hand, you will know that you have a firm foundation, that no matter what happens, you can trust in yourself, that you are fully capable of challenging the universe and approaching it on your own terms.

When you have completed the construction of your disk, you should wrap it in silk, preferably colored green (or black will do in a pinch). The reason why we wrap things in silk is that it is traditionally considered to be an excellent psychic insulator. In the same way that rubber is an insulator against electrical current, silk is supposedly an insulator against magical currents. Wrapping your instruments in silk means that they will be protected against stray influences which may affect them when they are not being used.

The next weapon we will obtain is the magical sword, or dagger. Now some authorities, including Crowley, hold that the sword and dagger should be two different weapons, used for different purposes, but personally I think that this is nitpicking. The only real difference between a dagger and a sword is in the size—what we are fundamentally talking about is an instrument for cutting with, and in this case at least, size isn't important. I will use the words sword and dagger interchangeably throughout the rest of this section. (Experienced Thelemic magicians may object that Crowley explicitly stated in several places that the sword and the dagger were two different weapons belonging to different systems, for example in his letter to Grady McMurtry of 25 September 1945. This is true, but I take as my justification Liber B vel Magi verse 9, which states that the third weapon of the magician is the Dagger. I am a Thelemite, not a Crowleyite.)

The dagger represents the element of Air. Like the Air, the sword penetrates all things, and it contains the power of life and death over us.

The sword is the analytical faculty of the brain; it is the instrument that cuts through the mass of disconnected facts, destroying that which is unnecessary, until only the important things remain. The scientific process is, at heart, a destructive process, not a constructive one, which probably comes as some surprise to the reader. A short reading course in the philosophy of science (with special reference to the ideas of Karl Popper) will correct this. Our critical faculties subdue the egoistic complexes in our minds in the way that the sword subdues the evil demons which threaten to invade our magick circle.

The dagger or sword should be cross-shaped—a straight, two-edged blade with a plain cross-handle. The blade is best made of steel (iron is the metal of Mars, god of War), and the handle can be anything you desire. A copper handle is good, copper being the metal of Venus, showing that violence must always be under the control of love. A wooden handle is also good, however, and perhaps simpler.

Traditionally, magicians should make the dagger themselves, forge the blade, carve the handle, etc., but this is beyond most people. It could be argued that the dedicated aspirant should be willing to learn, and the skills learned by going through the whole process are very valuable. The pride in knowing that the weapon has been made solely by you is a wonderful sensation. Personally I know of only one magician who has made his dagger from scratch—I watched him work on it for weeks, learning ancient metallurgic techniques and constructing his own forge in the backyard—and I have to confess the dagger he made really is a tremendous instrument. However, for most people the easiest solution is just to buy one.

Buying a dagger is not difficult—any camping shop will have a good selection. As usual, the simpler the better. Check that the blade has no engraving on it already—it should be plain steel. If you see a knife that you really know is right for you, but it has (for example) a large maker's mark on the blade, it is possible to cover the mark with careful use of an engraving tool at home; this is tricky work though, and I don't recommend it. Buying a large sword is not so easy, but you can pick up excellent oriental swords in antique shops; unfortunately these tend to have curved blades, which are generally not so good. Again, a lot depends on personal taste. One thing to keep in mind is that carrying large blade weapons around in the street is illegal in most places, and you can end up in prison if you're stopped by an unfriendly policeman (and most policemen are unfriendly to occultists). So if you're going to be performing rituals away from home either stick to a nice small innocent-looking knife or disguise your broadsword very well. A guitar case is perfect for this, especially if you are a long-haired weird looking sort of person anyway. Carrying a guitar case will make you look harmless, but strapping an exposed Japanese katana to your back—no way, dude. You'd be lucky to make it as far as the bus stop.

Once you've got your dagger, preparing it is easy. You just have to name it. All magick swords have names— Excalibur being probably the most famous example. With the disk, you had to think of a design that represented the universe. For the name of your sword, you must think of a word that represents the universe. This word can be anything that takes your fancy—but I suggest you go through a similar process of meditation as you went through when designing your disk. This time it's a little harder, since you cannot combine words in the same way that you could combine geometrical figures before. A good place to start is to use the linguistic equivalent of geometrical designs, which are Words of Power. You have already come across some of these during the pentagram ritual and during your mantra practice. Words such as TAO or ABRAHADABRA are excellent choices, but you should try to find out as much as possible about these words before choosing one. Crowley's *Magick in Theory and Practice* has several chapters dealing with magical formulas such as these. For all my own magical swords and daggers, I have found their names by bibliomancy. This is a simple process. You pick a book, preferably one with strong spiritual meaning to you—Liber AL is ideal, though the best is *The Holy Books of Thelema*. You concentrate deeply on your sword, and call on the gods to show you its name. Then let the book fall open at random, and the first word that your eye chances upon, that is the name. Although this might seem too simple, I have obtained excellent (and quick!) results with it every time.

Now that you have the name, it's time to get out the engraving tool or paintbrushes again. Put the name on the blade, near the hilt. Do not engrave anything else—just this one word. As you apply the name, feel the weapon in your hand responding to its new identity—you should realize that you are imbuing it with life, with its own personality. As this personality flows from you, the sword should always feel comfortable in your hand, it is only fully alive when you grasp it. When you are not using your dagger, wrap it in silk of yellow or sky-blue.

WARNING: blade weapons *are* weapons, and as such are dangerous! You do not have to have the blade of your sword sharp—you are unlikely to ever need to do any real physical cutting with it. I strongly advise that all magical blades be blunted before use; it won't make any difference to the magick you perform, and it's much, much safer. If you simply *must* have a sharp blade, then do not use a large sword unless you *really* know what you are doing. Keep all blade weapons in a scabbard when not in use—do not carry a naked blade stuck in your belt. If you are working with other people, *never* hold the blade outstretched while you are moving, unless you have given the others clear warning beforehand, and move very slowly. Do not make sudden movements at any time—even if someone else is holding the sword. Remember these things are specifically engineered to kill people, and they are extremely efficient at doing so. *I am not exaggerating!* Be careful! I once had to be rushed off in an ambulance and get several stitches in my hand when I was impaled on a sharp blade during a magical ritual, so I speak from personal experience.

The third of our magical weapons is the cup, symbol of the element of Water. This is obviously not very difficult to obtain and not even too difficult to make if you have a pottery class running near where you live. The cup ideally should be of the old-fashioned goblet type and made of silver. Silver goblets are, I know, quite expensive, but worth every penny, because they can be very beautiful, and beauty is one of the major qualities of the cup. As the sword is a weapon of War, the cup is an instrument of Love. It is a very feminine symbol, receptive, full of nourishment. Although it is essentially passive, never forget that Water, too, is strong and forceful. Meditate on how the rocks by the seashore are gradually worn down by the waves. The strength of Water is a feminine strength, a strength that lies buried in mysterious depths, but never gives up.

By now, you know that each weapon must in some way encapsulate your vision of the universe, and the cup is no different in this respect. What you will now do is find a *number* which in some way represents the universe. Perhaps you see the universe as a huge unity, so the number 1 would fit. Or perhaps you recognize that everything in the world is dual, positive and negative, so 2 seems more appropriate. Or the number 11, being the number of the goddess Nuit: "My number is 11, as all their numbers who are of us"—Liber AL. The number 4 you already know to be the number of the elements, of things manifested on the Earth, so perhaps this is also good. Just like you could combine geometrical figures to make the design for your disk, you can combine numbers for the cup. You do this by multiplication. For example, 11 is the number of Thelemic magick, and 4 is the number of manifestation. So if you want to symbolize the manifestation of Thelemic magick on your cup, you would multiply 4 x 11 = 44. Note that numerological systems work by multiplication not by addition and subtraction as is often believed. As usual, meditate carefully for a few days to find a number that really fits perfectly.

So it's back to the engraving tool to put a number on the bottom of your cup, and hey presto, it's finished. Not so difficult. Wrap it in deep blue or silver silk, and lay it on your altar.

The fourth and final elemental weapon is the most important of all: the magick wand. The wand is the symbol of Fire, of the primal basic energy that flows through all life. The cup is Love, the wand is Will; together: "Love under Will." The wand is an extension of your hand, of your ability to reach out and manipulate the world around you. To understand the full function of the wand, meditate on the conductor of a symphony orchestra with his baton and also on the first scene of Kubrick's movie *2001*, when the protohumans learn to pick up sticks to use as clubs. In both cases you are seeing the wand in action, and it is important that you understand that it is essentially the *same* action. It is the Will extended into reality.

Of all the magical weapons, the wand is the easiest to make by oneself, and I do recommend in this case that you do so.

Traditionally you should cut a branch from a tree and carve it into shape. I know many magicians who have done this, and the results are excellent. If you're going to do it, get a hatchet and go for a long walk in the woods. Find a nice tree that appeals to you, preferably ash or hazel. If you can't tell one tree from another, get a book that tells you or a friend who lives in the country. Cut off, with one stroke if you can manage it (you probably won't be able to), a branch a little bit longer than your forearm. Before you cut, be sure to touch the tree's trunk and commune with the life inside. Say a prayer to the spirit of the tree, and ask for its permission to take part of its life to help you in your work. If you get the feeling that the tree is not happy to give up one of its branches, do not take it but go to another tree instead. This is most important. Trees are among the most vibrant living creatures on the planet, but their movement is so slow that we often forget this. You must ensure that you respect the tree whose branch you want to have. Some magicians prefer to get the wood for their wand in the autumn. If you walk in the woods frequently at this time, you can find a branch which has just fallen and has not yet begun to rot. This branch has no karma attached to it, but will not have the fullness of life that a branch cut from a living tree will have.

Once you have your branch, take it home and begin to carve it into shape. Try to get it as straight as possible, but also try to go with the natural flow of the wood. Trim the length so that it is the same as the length from your elbow to the tip of your middle finger.

If you don't want all the hassle of going through the previous procedure, you can just go down to your local hardware store and buy a length of wood dowel rod. Again try to get ash or hazel. Measure the distance from your elbow to middle fingertip before you leave home—this makes things a little easier in the shop! Doweling is nicely straight and round, and perfectly adequate (my favorite wand was made this way).

While you're in the hardware shop, get a pair of metal or rubber ferrules. A ferrule is a cap which fits over the end of a walking stick to stop the wood from splitting or otherwise being damaged. Metal is better, but I've used rubber ones before, and oddly enough they work quite well. At home, fit these to each end of your wand.

Many magicians like to decorate their wands with mystic inscriptions, and although this can look fantastic, for now I don't recommend it. As always, I advise simplicity. What you should do, however, is get some good magical oil—the best is Abra-melin oil, available from occult supply shops, but an essential oil like sandalwood will also do. Put on an apron or some old clothes, then place a few drops of oil in the palm of one hand. Take the wand in your other hand, and begin to rhythmically rub the oil into the wood. While you are doing this, repeat a mantra, either internally or out loud. You should try to keep this up for at least half an hour. Do it every day for at least a week, preferably more like four weeks. Although it might seem like a great deal of work, it's actually quite easy, because you can do it while you are watching TV or even while having a conversation with friends. The mantra practice that you have been doing for the last few weeks should have given you the ability to keep reciting the mantra while concentrating on something else.

After you have been anointing the wand for some days, it will have become softer and smell very sweet all the time, but what is more important, it will have become totally part of you and will feel like an extension of yourself, which after all, is what it is. I have a wand that I anointed like this for about an hour every day for three months, and now, ten years later, it still smells of the oil. The oil will also protect the wood and help keep it clean—unoiled wood will spoil over time.

Wrap your wand in a square of red silk, since it is the weapon of Fire. You will now meditate on the wand and work out an *action* which represents the universe for you. This is tricky, but if you keep the rules for the previous weapons in mind, it should not be impossible. The combination of simple gestures into one action or sequence of actions is an obvious way of approaching this. You can think of gestures that convey certain meanings—the gestures which you perform to draw the pentagram, to take a very overtly magical example. A more day-to-day gesture, but still very magically significant, might be the "Thumbs up" sign. The signs of Ra-Hoor-Khuit and Hoor-paar-kraat are signs that you know well by now (I hope), so perhaps these would be useful. As always, *you* must decide what will best transmit your view of the universe. I know a professional musician whose wand action consisted in his taking it on stage every night during a tour and using it to signal the beginning of the concert.

The wand is a totally active instrument. It represents basic raw energy, and it is fully part of your being, so do not place a mark upon it unlike the other weapons. So how do you fit your chosen action to the wand? You will perform this action when you come to consecrate your weapons, which is what comes next in the process.

You should have acquired a complete set of magical weapons by now, but although you have infused them with your own personal power during the process of making and engraving them, magically speaking the weapons are still inert—they contain no divine energy, only human energy. To become true magical weapons. they must be consecrated, which means that they must be dedicated to the gods and blessed by them. Only when this is done will the weapons be able to reach out beyond this plane and bring about effects in other spheres. So now you will perform an invocation, a calling down of the gods to the material plane.

You should have performed the pentagram ritual several times by now, so you already know that rituals should generally have a symmetrical form. In the pentagram rite you begin with the Cross of Light, then draw the pentagrams and invoke the gods Nuit and Hadit, then perform the Cross of Light again. A full invocation is essentially an expanded version of this process. First you begin with a pentagram ritual, then perform a middle section where you invoke the specific energies that you wish to contact, then finish with another complete pentagram rite. Symmetry within symmetry.

Your first banishing pentagram ritual gets rid of all the diverse forces whirling around your environment, leaving your circle as a sort of magical vacuum. Into this vacuum you can then draw down whichever god or goddess you desire and perform the magical act which you Will. Once this act is complete, you then perform a second banishing in order to make the atmosphere "neutral" once more. Some might argue that a second banishing should not be necessary, since the god you have invoked is likely to be one that is useful to you—therefore why banish it again? Granted, the god may well contain an energy that is very useful for the magician, but it will contain only a limited form of all the many varied energies that can exist. By allowing the influence of one god to predominate, you are reducing the potential influences of the other gods, and this is very dangerous indeed. No energy is good or bad in itself, as I keep on emphasizing, but unbalanced energy is not very productive.

In a similar vein, it is also important to realize that invoking the gods and goddesses that you personally find it easy to relate to is not—in the long-term—the best method of invocation. Although to the beginner especially, invoking a god that is close to one's own nature is much easier and more fulfilling, if you continue to do so, you will succeed in strengthening the parts of your psyche that are already strong, while allowing the weaker parts of your psyche to atrophy. So make sure that as you progress through your magical career, you invoke many different gods and goddesses, particularly those which you may not feel sympathetic to. In this way, you will begin to understand and develop parts of your consciousness which you may have previously avoided. Most especially, ensure that you at least occasionally invoke a divinity that is of another gender than yourself—and remember that gods come in three genders: female, male, and androgyne.

Enough digression, back to the ritual at hand. You are about to perform a ritual to consecrate your new magical weapons. As always, practical considerations come first. You should already have a temple area and a magical circle to work in. You will need a small altar preferably with a covering of some sort. On your altar you will place the weapons to be consecrated, plus a candle, a thurible, a book, and a bell. As you know, you should place more candles around the outside of the circle. Any number of candles will do, but eight is probably best for this rite.

The candles can be of any color that you desire really (there are various symbolic ideas behind each color, but for this rite it is not so important)—black candles have a nice gothic feel to them, as do red; white candles are easy to come by, but not quite as atmospheric. Use whatever you feel comfortable with, but do not use strangely shaped or multicolored "art" candles, stick to something simple and elegant.

A thurible is an incense holder, which is usually a container made of brass which contains a disk of charcoal, plus some incense. If you don't know where to get a proper thurible, a small brass or ceramic bowl will do. Half fill it with sand or earth before you light the charcoal, because this innocent-looking black charcoal disk will reach super hot temperatures and can do you some serious damage if it is not insulated. As with candle holders, make sure that the thurible is stable, and not too close to loose paper or fabric—don't set light to your temple! As for the incense that you will burn, there is an enormous amount of incense to choose from. Try to stay away from the typical New Age type zodiacal incenses—not only are they normally not very good, they are too specialized for this working. Perhaps a Mercury incense would do if you can find one. If you have contact with a specialist occult supply store, the best invocatory incense you can get is Abra-melin incense, which really is fantastic. Some occult suppliers now provide Temple of Thelema incense, which I can certainly recommend, since the original recipe was put together by Frater Marabo and myself at The Sorcerer's Apprentice shop in England. Your incense will probably come in a plastic bag, but you should store it in an airtight container at home; if left in a plastic bag, it will lose some of its potency after a while.

If you have no contact with a good occult supplier, you can get what you need at a Roman Catholic supply shop, of which there are many in the Western world. Christian altar incense, or frankincense, is absolutely fine, though it may have rather complex connotations for those who have been brought up in the bosom of the Church. One advantage of Roman Catholic supply shops is that the stuff is usually a great deal cheaper than at an occult supplier. But then you may not really want to give your money to them ...

At worst, the simplest solution of all is to use incense in the form of joss sticks or cones. These are not nearly as good as proper incense, but they will do at a pinch. Use a combination of jasmine and rose, an equal number of each.

The book on your altar should be the book which best expresses your magical aspirations for your life; it is the materialization of the divine Will. It should ideally be a book of inspired writing, i.e. writing that has come not from human ideas, but from the gods. For a Christian, this book would obviously be the Bible, for a Moslem, the Koran. Since we are dealing with Thelemic magick here, the book on your altar should be Liber AL vel Legis, since this is the foundation stone of all of what we have been doing. There are also several other Thelemic "Holy Books" which have been inspired by nonhuman sources, including Liber B, Liber Cheth, and Liber A'Ash; these three are reprinted in Appendix VII of *Magick in Theory and Practice,* so you can use this volume if you have no copy of Liber AL.

Your magick bell is what you will use to announce your presence during a ritual. It serves to punctuate the various parts of the ritual and to "wake up" the astral beings you will be dealing with. When you strike the bell, imagine that the resonances you set up are vibrating throughout the entire universe. Actually you don't have to imagine this, because it is literally true that any vibration you set up goes on to infinity. The magick bell should preferably be an oriental type of bell, which is more like a deep metal bowl with a low, long tone, but at a pinch any bell will do. A small dinner gong is very easy to come by and can be very effective indeed when set on your altar.

OK, now you have made all your external preparations, but you are still not ready to begin, for you must prepare yourself as well as preparing your temple. Before any important magical ritual you should fast, i.e., take no food for at least four hours or perhaps for a whole day if the ritual is really important. During this time, you may drink mineral water (tap water is generally not recommended—it usually contains too many impurities) or fruit juice or perhaps tea if the weather is cold. Coffee is not a good idea; you'll end up speeding out of your mind after a while. You should also be thinking about what you are about to do, getting your mind into an appropriate state. It is also best if you talk to others as little as possible during this time—switch off the telephone and computer. Just before you begin you should wash yourself all over; if possible, take a bath and add some scented magical oil. After your wash, do not put on your normal clothes, but wear your robes instead. From the moment you put on your robe, you put on your "magical personality." You are no longer Kim Smith, mild-mannered reporter, you are now Neophyte Magician Nemo, and when you enter your temple and stand before your altar, I guarantee that you will feel quite different than you ever have before (you'll probably feel damn silly if you catch sight of yourself in the mirror, but never mind, we all do at first).

Now unwrap your new magical weapons and lay them on the altar. You should pour some water into the Cup. Then sprinkle a little salt in the water—sea salt is best. Light the candles and the incense disk (I bet you forgot to bring a lighter), and when the charcoal is glowing, add a good portion of incense. All is ready.

THE CONSECRATION OF THE MAGUS

Begin the working with the pentagram ritual. Then, facing East, pick up the bell and strike it slowly eleven times, in the rhythm 1-3-3-3-1. Put down the bell, and make the sign of Rending the Veil, then intone the words:

I declare this temple open in the name of Ra-Hoor-Khuit.

Pick up your Disk, and holding it up vertically in front of you in both hands, say:

I proclaim that my holy place shall be untouched throughout the centuries.

Laying down the Disk, pick up your Dagger and hold it in both hands, outstretched before you, pointing slightly downward. Visualize the tip glowing with solar energy. Now turn slowly widdershins (to your left), and draw a burning circle of force around you. When you have completed the circle and are again facing East, lower the dagger and loudly say:

Bahlasti! Ompehda!

In the name of the Mighty and Terrible One, I proclaim that I have banished the Shells unto their habitations.

Exchange the Dagger for the Cup. Holding it in one hand, dip the thumb of the other hand in the water. With your thumb make a cross on your forehead, then make a circle around the cross.

Put down the Cup, and lift your Wand. Hold it vertically erect in front of you, with both hands clasped around the shaft, fingers interlaced, before your chest. Proclaim your magical intention:

I [your name] have come to this holy place to achieve the consecration of my magical weapons.

Lay down the Wand, and make the sign of Isis Mourning. Pause in this position for a moment, breathing slowly and deeply.

Pick up the Disk, and advance to the East. Visualize the form of a large male lion outside the circle, with glowing golden skin and a mane of shining, shaggy hair. He stands on a verdant savanna, and his royal bearing proclaims that he rules all the world and all that lives within it. Show him the design on the Disk which represents the universe. As he sees it, he lets out a huge roar, and his breath fills the Disk with the powers of the Earth. Roar out his name in return:

Therion!

Laying down the Disk, pick up the Dagger, and advance to the North. Visualize the night sky and the body of the Goddess of Space. Hold up the Dagger in both hands by the blade, hilt upward, forming an upright cross before you. Speak the name of the Dagger, that represents the universe. The goddess bends down to you and kisses the Dagger, filling it with the powers of Air. Say her name:

Nuit.

Return to the altar and exchange the Dagger for the Cup. Advance to the West, and visualize the figure of a beautiful, voluptuous, naked, red-haired woman. Hold the Cup up to her with both hands, and speak the number that represents the universe. She reaches out toward you and strokes the Cup with the tips of her fingers, filling it with the powers of Water. Whisper her name:

Babalon.

Going back to the altar, put down the Cup and take up the Wand. Advance to the South, and see before you a ball of fire, with a huge pair of wings unfolding from it, and within the flames a serpent coiled. Perform the action by which the Wand represents the universe; at the finish of the action hold the Wand outstretched in front of you. The serpent leaps from the flames, tongue outstretched, and spits venom over the Wand, filling it with the powers of Fire. Bellow his name:

Hadit!

Return to the East and, still holding the Wand clasped before you, perform the Call (at each "Thee, Thee I invoke," make the sign of Apophis):

(I)

I invoke Hermes, the Lord of Wisdom and of Utterance, the god that cometh forth from the Veil.

(A)

O Thou! Majesty of Godhead! Wisdom-crowned Hermes!

Lord of the Gates of the Universe! Thee, Thee I invoke!

Thou who art Spirit and Matter, thou who art Peace and Power! Thee, Thee I invoke!

Thou who wieldest the Wand of Power! Thee, Thee I invoke!

Thou whose Word is the Will of the Gods! Thee, Thee I invoke!

(O)

Behold! I am Yesterday, To-Day, and the Brother of To-Morrow!

I am born again and again.

Mine is the Unseen Force, whereof the gods are sprung! Which is as Life unto the Dwellers in the Watch-Towers of the Universe.

I am the Charioteer of the East, Lord of the Past and of the Future.

I see by mine own inward light: Lord of Resurrection; Who cometh forth from the Dusk, and my birth is from the House of Death.

KRATOS!

Approach the altar, and reverse the Wand so that it points downward. Plunge it into the Cup, with the words:

With the Wand createth He.

Moving deosil (to your right), bring the Wand to the Southern quarter and lay it on the floor, inside the circle. Then continue deosil until you are once more facing East. Take up the Cup, and pour a drop of water on to the blade of the Dagger, saying:

With the Cup preserveth he.

Move deosil again, and lay the Cup in the West. Returning deosil to the East, take up the Dagger, and holding it point down, strike the Disk, saying:

With the Dagger destroyeth He.

Go deosil once more and take the Dagger to the

North, then return to the East. Take up the Disk, and press it once to your forehead, once to your lips, lastly once to your breast and say:

With the Coin redeemeth He.

Lay down the disk on the floor in the East, then stand in the center of the circle. Make the Sign of Osiris Risen, saying:

His weapons fulfill the wheel.

Strike the Bell eleven times in the rhythm 3-5-3. Perform the pentagram ritual once more, then finish the working with the sign of Closing the Veil, saying:

I declare this temple closed in the name of Ra-Hoor-Khuit.

Clap your hands once together, hard and loud, then stamp your feet on the floor a few times. Blow out the candles, and wrap your newly consecrated weapons in their coverings. The rite is finished.

Notes on the Ritual of Consecration

The bell is struck after the pentagram ritual in order to announce the transition from this material plane to the spiritual plane. It is struck eleven times, since eleven is the number of magick (as you are probably aware by now, after your studies on the Cup).

The sign of Rending the Veil is made by holding your hands in front of your chest, with the backs of the hands touching, then moving them apart as if pulling apart a pair of curtains (see page 116 for sign figures). The sign shows that you are now stepping across the line which normally divides us from the astral world and that as a magician you affirm your right to gaze upon that which is hidden from the sight of the great mass of humanity. The corollary to the sign of

Rending the Veil is the sign of Closing the Veil which you perform at the end of the rite. This sign consists of holding your
arms stretched out to each side of you, hands balled into
loose fists, and moving them together, just as if you are closing a pair of curtains.

You now declare the temple open in the name of Ra-
Hoor-Khuit. You use his name because he is the Lord of magick in this Aeon. All your temple workings will be under his
auspices, regardless of which god or goddess you may be
invoking. He is your guide and protector each time you enter
the circle.

In the next section of the rite, you perform a sort of sec-
ondary banishing and consecration of yourself. The Disk here
is used as a shield, to protect you from harm, and the Dagger
as an armament to menace your enemies. The words
"Bahlasti" and "Ompehda" are very powerful Words of Banishing from Liber AL that will drive away harmful influences.
The water from the Cup consecrates you when you place it on
your forehead; the cross within the circle sign you know, of
course; by using this figure you affirm your dedication to the
Thelemic magical current. You hold the Wand while stating
your magical intention because the Wand is the representation of your Will. You can easily use this whole section of the
ritual in future workings, since it serves to "set you up" for
the invocation that comes next. Of course, you should alter
the wording of the Wand section depending on what your
magical intention is for each particular working.

The sign of Isis Mourning is made by raising the right
hand, palm facing forward, and lowering the left hand, palm
facing back. Take your weight on your left foot, and move
your right foot back a little, balancing on the toes. Lower
your head and turn it slightly to the left. Note that you do *not*
reverse these directions if you are left-handed. This sign represents the outflowing current of nature and of aspiration
toward the divine spirit.

The figure of the lion in the Eastern quarter is a representation of Therion, who is the living personification of the

Rending the Veil

Closing the Veil

Isis Mourning

Apophis

Osiris Risen

Thelemic Current. East is the quarter of Earth, and the lion is the Lord of the Earth. Remember that you can see Therion depicted in the tarot card XI Lust, where he is shown in seven-headed form. If you prefer, you can use this form when you visualize him, though it may be a little harder to do at first. His roar is the vehicle of his power, for he is the Logos of the Aeon (*Logos* is Greek for Word). As Lord of nature, his Word is Law, and his Law is Liberty.

By now you should need no introduction to the goddess Nuit, Our Lady of Night. She sends her power through her kiss, for her Word is Love.

In the West is the goddess Babalon, the goddess of sexuality, the Virgin Whore. She receives all who come to her in purity. She is a goddess without shame; she is Woman unrestrained, no longer bound by mortal convention; she is proud and fierce in her sensuality. She strokes the Cup, and it is filled with Life.

In the Southern quarter is Hadit. He is "the flame that burns in every heart of man and in the core of every star;" he is the point of light within that moves all things. Thus he is represented as a ball of primal fiery energy, the fuel of all that lives, with beating wings to show his power of movement. The serpent within is the inspiration, the sudden striking spark of illumination that destroys all illusion. He spits venom on the Wand, imbuing it with the power of Light.

Now you return to the East and invoke Hermes. This part of the ritual is really the crux of the whole operation, since it is at this time that you are actually calling the divine power down inside yourself, not just into your instruments. There are three sections to this Call, referred to as I, A, and O, these letters standing for Isis, Apophis, and Osiris. You will meet this formula of IAO often during your magical work in the future, especially during invocations. For now, there is no need to worry too much about the meaning of IAO—it will become clearer to you as time (and this book) goes on.

In the first (Isis) section, the magician addresses the god in the third person form of speech: "I invoke Hermes ... (etc.)." In the second (Apophis) section, the god is drawn closer, and addressed directly, in the second person: "O Thou ... Thee, Thee I invoke!" In the final (Osiris) section, the god is addressed in the first person, because the magician and the god are now one unity: "I am Yesterday, To-Day and the Brother of To-Morrow!"

Study this point well; it is vital that you fully understand the process that is occurring here. Unless the god is brought inside you, you do not have the ability to perform your magick. Remember that a Thelemite does not pray on bended knee to an uncaring external god, the Thelemite becomes god, fully and literally. The sign of Apophis you know by now from the Nu-Sphere ritual—fling your arms upward and outward, forming a V shape. Just as you did then, you make it to show that you destroy the god—that is, that you destroy the illusion that the god is a separate being outside of you; you destroy the Image of the god, for you will become the god.

Hermes is the Greek god of magick and speech, and as such is similar to the Roman Mercury and the Egyptian Tahuti (Thoth). He is pictured as a young man wearing winged sandals and carrying a Caduceus (a wand with two snakes entwined around it—a common international symbol for doctors and healers). He is obviously the patron god of all magicians and, despite his love of tricks and jokes, is a god who can be very helpful in ritual workings, giving his power freely and kindly to those who seek after it. He is a very creative god, full of life and energy, and whirling, fast motion. You can see him in his classical form in Atu I, the tarot card of the Magus.

As you recite this invocation, the visualizations that you perform are of paramount importance. At the beginning, you should see Hermes as a faint universal presence, moving at blinding speed through the cosmos. As you move into the second part of the Call, visualize him becoming more solid, floating above you and around you, and appeal directly to him. You should feel him begin to acknowledge your presence as you speak. Speak slowly and clearly, but forcefully, and allow plenty of time for the force to build up within you. As you move into the third part of the Call, you should experience the god moving right inside your body, and simultaneously feel your whole being expand and become godlike. Visualize your aura transfigured into the form of Hermes, feel yourself flying through space and time (your practice in assuming god-forms should come in very useful now).

Allow time for the identification to become complete, and at that moment when you feel completely unified with Hermes, utter the word KRATOS. This is a Word of Power particularly associated with the creative force of this god. It is hard to describe exactly what this moment of divine possession is like—it is, by definition, beyond rational thought. It is to magick what an orgasm is to sex (read this sentence again carefully—it does *not* mean that divine possession is the *same* as an orgasm). When you utter KRATOS, it should come out in a similar sort of fashion as that of a cry of sexual ecstasy, almost as if it is being forced out against your conscious control. The word should spring from the deepest recesses of your soul, directly from the point of light inside you that we call the Starry Nature. In this way the divinity inside unites with the divinity outside.

So you can see that in our invocations the magician does not control the god, or the god take over the Will of the magician, contrary to popular belief. The relationship between god and magician is one of Love, of two things uniting to form a new being. "There is no bond that can unite the divided but love" (Liber AL I, 41). Both the god and the magician are perfect beings, but in their union they become something else, something that transcends all boundaries, something which is the resultant of the Will of the magician and the Power of the god. "The Perfect and the Perfect are one Perfect and not two" (AL I, 45).

Now that you have the god's force within you, you can go on to consecrate your weapons fully. Note that previously you used the weapons in the order, Disk, Dagger, Cup, Wand, moving from Earth to Air to Water to Fire, onward and upward toward the realm of Spirit; the realm where you made your invocation of Hermes. Now it is time to bring the power back down to Earth, so now you go in the reverse order, Wand, Cup, Dagger, Disk.

At the end, you press the Disk to your own body; to the forehead, symbol of your vision (spiritual vision, that is—the third eye, Ajna chakra); your lips, symbol of your speech; and to your heart, symbol of your love. By this act, you are bringing the power full circle, from you (the god), transmuted through your weapons, back to you (the magician). You have formed a circuit, rather like an electrical circuit, through which the power flows— "His weapons fulfil the wheel." You give the sign of Osiris Risen, for you have died as a human and been reborn as a god; the cycle of nature, of death and rebirth has taken place, the wheel has been fulfilled.

(Note for further meditation: TARO = the Magical Book of Thoth/Hermes, ROTA = a wheel)

By going through the weapons with the four symbolic actions, you are transferring the power of Hermes from one weapon to the other, while simultaneously linking all four of the elemental powers into one unified whole. The phrases that you use while doing this are from the Thelemic Holy Book called Liber B vel Magi, which deals particularly with the Magus and his weapons. For this reason the phraseology used should not be changed from "He," even if you are currently manifested on Earth in a female body. The "He" that is referred to here is not you the human magician, it is the divine "He," Hermes, the Magus; that is, you as the god.

FURTHER STUDY

Magick—Appendix VII: Liber A vel Armorum
Magick—Appendix VII: Liber B vel Magi
Magick Without Tears—Chapter 23: Improvising a Temple

CHAPTER NINE

MAGICAL MODELS

By now in your Thelemic career you should be starting to learn quite a bit about the basic ideas behind magical practice. In fact, you have probably learned just enough to begin to get really confused about how everything actually hangs together. As I have continually emphasized throughout the course of this book, life is complex, and we are dealing here with the study of energies that are not only extremely subtle but also extremely powerful and wide ranging. It is easy to get very lost in all these complexities. Sooner or later, the budding magician (that's you) must begin to build up a classification system, a magical filing cabinet, which can hold all this data in a convenient and "user-friendly" form.

Over the centuries occultists have developed several systems for storing their learning, the most widespread of which is known as the Qabalah (sometimes spelled Kabbalah—Hebrew doesn't use the Roman alphabet, so neither transliteration is more "correct" than the other really). The Qabalah was derived originally from ancient medieval Jewish sources, but it has continually evolved as magicians have added to our store of occult knowledge until now it has become an enormous repository of arcane lore. This probably makes you think that if it's so big, it must be really difficult to learn, but it's really quite the opposite—the Qabalah in essence is a very simple diagram that one can easily draw on one sheet of paper. This diagram is known as the Tree of Life (see page 122).

Let's have a look at the shape of this Tree of Life. It is composed of an arrangement of circles, joined by lines. Well, sort of. Since it is really a three-dimensional figure that has been drawn on a two-dimensional page, it would be more accurate to say that the Tree of Life is made up of spheres, or balls, connected by tubular paths. (Yes, the next time that someone tells you that magick is just a load of balls you can

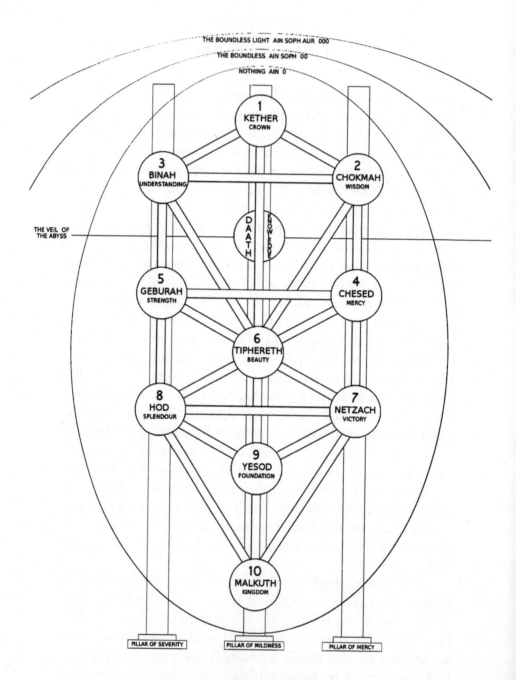

THE TREE OF LIFE

tell them that they're right.) Study the shape of the Tree of Life carefully for a few minutes; then close your eyes and try to visualize the Tree of Life standing in front of you in three dimensions. Think of it as being a real tree, a Christmas tree upon whose branches you will hang all the wonderful presents that your magical training will bring to you. This is an exercise that will be very useful for you to incorporate into your regular meditation practice for the future.

Since our magical Tree of Life has grown from Jewish roots, you will often hear of its parts being referred to by their Jewish names—just as in yoga we tend to use Sanskrit technical terms, in Qabalah we tend to use Hebrew terms. The Hebrew word for a sphere of the Tree of Life is Sephirah (plural: Sephiroth), and you will come across this term frequently. I'll probably use both Hebrew and English interchangeably, since it really doesn't matter which language we use, the concept that we refer to is still the same.

Let's look at the Tree again in a little more detail. You can see that we have eleven spheres (obviously, since eleven is the number of magick—I think that it's safe to assume that you've learned that by now!). One of the spheres is slightly different from the others, usually being drawn with a dotted line instead of a solid one, but we'll come to why that is later. First let's just look at the pattern. The Spheres are arranged in three columns, a long column in the middle with a shorter one on each side. These columns are called the Pillars of the Tree of Life and provide the stability for the whole Tree, like the pillars that hold up a temple. The Pillars to either side of the Tree provide the dynamic energies which drive the system, while the Middle Pillar provides the harmony which balances these opposing forces. The whole diagram is a model of the progression of the forces which are at work in our universe at any one time.

Above the diagram of the Sephiroth you can see three curved lines, labeled Ain, Ain Soph, and Ain Soph Aur (in English: Nothing, The Boundless, and The Boundless Light). These three lines are called the Three Veils of the Absolute.

Beyond them lies—well, something that neither I nor you can describe, by definition. In fact to even say that it is *something* at all is wrong. As Liber AL puts it:

> ... speak not of thee as One, but as None; and let them speak not of thee at all, since thou art continuous!

What lies beyond the Three Veils of the Absolute is the Absolute IT: that which we have symbolized by the goddess Nuit, since words cannot even begin to describe what "IT" is.

Yet Nuit gradually manifests herself through these Three Veils and eventually becomes the known Universe. The first manifestation is as a point in space, and this is symbolized by the first Sephirah of the Tree of Life. This first Sphere is the topmost one of the Tree and is called Kether, meaning the Crown. It is number 1 of the series; it is pure white light as it is the primary source of all within the manifested universe. As such it has many of the qualities of the god Hadit—can you begin to see already how this simple diagram contains our magical learning within it?

Now imagine the force thus created spreading outward, to form all things. Nuit has split herself to create Hadit, and the interplay between them creates what the ancient Daoists called the Yang and the Yin; that is, the primeval male and female energies. These form the next two Spheres. Sephirah number 2 is called Chokmah, or Wisdom. As Hadit plays with Nuit in their eternal cosmic Love, the entire concept of "Twoness" becomes manifest. If at first there is None, then there is None and One, immediately we get the idea that there are now two things. Where Kether is a point of light, Chokmah is a line of radiance, the connection of two things that have become separate, and the direction of the movement between them. Chokmah is the first Wisdom, the first sign of the desire of Hadit to perform his Will. But as it has not the pure brilliance of Kether, the color of Chokmah has become grey.

The third Sephirah is called Binah, meaning Understanding. As the first Will becomes real, as the Yang energy becomes manifest in the universe, simultaneously the Yin, or basic female energy, must also come into being to balance it. Since all things come from the first division of Nothingness into two parts (Nuit and Hadit), so must all energies balance. For every positive energy there must be an equivalent negative energy—for each contains the seed of the other within it. As the Will arises, the Understanding grows to enfold it. As Kether is symbolized by a point, and Chokmah by a line, Binah is symbolized by a triangle, the simplest bounded figure in geometry. Chokmah is often referred to as the Great Father of All, so Binah is the Great Mother. In Chokmah we find the divine force of Therion, the primal force of the Will, and in Binah, Our Lady Babalon, who receives Him, who receives all impressions, all desires. Since she takes in all light, the color of Binah is therefore black.

From the interplay of these energies come the lower Sephiroth. Yet no longer do we have the purity of Nuit and Hadit and of Therion and Babalon, for their children are a mixture of the pure Yin and Yang energies. All that springs from them are hybrids, crossbreeds, who have lost the essential qualities of their parents. So here in the Tree we have a veil, splitting the three highest Spheres from the lower Spheres. This veil is called the Veil of the Abyss, for this is a huge gulf that separates the lower from the higher.

I think that here I should ask you to pause, perhaps reread the preceding paragraphs, and spend some time meditating on these ideas. It is important that you should understand what has been said above before we proceed further down the Tree. These three uppermost Spheres, called the Supernals, are the basic forces that create all the others. As Lao Zi says in the Dao De Jing:

"The Dao formulated the One. The One exhaled the Two. The Two were parents of the Three. The Three were parents of all things. All things pass from Obscurity to Manifestation, inspired harmoniously by the Breath of the Void."

Right, back to the Tree. Hanging suspended in the Abyss

is a mysterious "invisible" Sephirah called Da'ath, which means Knowledge. This Sphere is not number 4, as you might think. It is number 11. On many diagrams of the Tree of Life, it is even left out altogether. Da'ath is knowledge, logic, thought processes. It is the first manifestation of duality in the sense that it is the first confused child of the Supernals. In the modern society that we live in, many of us have been taught that Knowledge is an end to itself, but you should remember that Knowledge is not the same thing as Understanding, or Wisdom. Wisdom is the capability of determining the right course of action and performing that action. Understanding is the capacity of comprehending the actions of others and relating to those actions. But Knowledge—that is perception without emotion, comprehension without movement, thought in isolation from deeper roots. It is the false crown of Ego that tries to hide us from Kether, the true Crown of the Will. It is a confused child that knows that it is lost, but has no Understanding of the way home or Wisdom to seek the way.

Da'ath has no god attributed to it; instead it is the home of the demon Choronzon, the demon which lies, argues, debates, and confuses aspirants, and in the end tears them apart. Unlike the other Spheres of the Tree, Da'ath has no color attributed to it—Da'ath is too full of confusion to have any attributes at all. I suppose it could be symbolized by the spectrum, the pure white light of Kether split up into its separate component parts by the power of Knowledge. The fabled Rainbow Bridge of Norse mythology, which links the material world with the world of the divine, is an obvious symbol of Da'ath.

The way that I have just described Da'ath makes it all sound a little bit "evil," but beware of so thinking! No Sephirah can be good or bad in itself—all are simple universal forces and as such are completely important and necessary without moral value. As well as being the source of confusion, Da'ath is also the bridge to the Supernal Triad; it is through Da'ath that the Supernal energies flow into the

Sephiroth below. As Thelemic magicians we are Gnostics—and Gnosis means Knowledge! Only through Knowledge can we gain to the Supernals.

This is a great and holy secret of magick: the energy that we use comes from Chaos. It is only by directing it with our True Wills that we order it into the patterns that we need. Without Understanding and Wisdom, our magick must always end in confusion. Da'ath is the only Sephirah that has no paths to connect it to the rest of the Tree—it is we as magicians that must create those paths in ourselves.

The fourth Sphere of the Tree of Life lies on the right-hand Pillar below Chokmah and is called Chesed, meaning Mercy. In Chesed we see the first formulation of the material world. Thus the geometrical figure of Chesed is the cube, the primal three-dimensional figure. As you already know from your previous work, four is always the number of stability, of setting energy in place. This is the job of the Sphere of Mercy. The gods of Chesed are thus gods who are creator, builder gods, and gods that rule the material universe through their belief in stability. The Roman god Jupiter is a perfect example of this, or indeed the Judeo-Christian Jehovah. Since these gods are mainly gods that live in the sky, the obvious color of the Sphere is blue.

This conservatism of Chesed must always give rise to its opposite, for where there is an excess of stability, there will always be a violent revolutionary force attempting to break it down. This is the next Sephirah, called Geburah, or Strength. Geburah is energetic, always moving and destroying. Its symbol is the pentagram, the Star of Force and Fire. Where there is Geburah, there is blood; thus its color is red. The gods of Geburah are the gods of war—like the Roman Mars.

The conjunction of these two Spheres is bound to be a difficult one. We have brought into being the first true duality. Above the Abyss, among the Supernal Triad of Kether, Chokmah, and Binah, there is harmony. But below the Abyss we are no longer dealing with the purity of Yin and Yang. The energies have been polluted by confusion. To harmonize these violently opposing forces we need a new child, and this is the next, central Sphere of the Tree, which is Tiphareth, Beauty.

In the triad of Chesed, Geburah, and Tiphareth, we have a reflection of the Supernal Triad, and unlike Da'ath, Tiphareth has a path directly connecting it to Kether, the Crown of the system. It is the only Sphere below the Abyss to have this connection. The job of Tiphareth is to harmonize all things. It is the child of Chesed and Geburah and balances their forces; thus its color is yellow, so that in this central triad of Sephiroth we have the three primary colors of blue, red, and yellow—from the combination of these primary colors, all other colors may be formed. Tiphareth is the center of the whole Tree, taking the energy of Kether and giving it to the other Spheres. It is symbolized by the Holy Hexagram, the six-pointed star, which links the triangle of the divine with the triangle of man. It is like the Sun in our solar system, the central point around which all revolve and draw light. All Sun gods are sacred to Tiphareth, gods like Apollo, Mithras, Osiris, even Jesus Christ, gods that die and are reborn, as the sun dies each evening and is born anew each morning.

Again I advise the reader to pause here for a moment and meditate on this triad. Picture it in your mind as a three-dimensional figure in front of you. Concentrate on each of the Spheres in turn, understand their functions and how they work together in harmony. See how they reflect the Supernal Triad after another manner. Only when you have done this should you move on to the lower triad.

The seventh Sephirah is Netzach, which in English means Victory. Here we begin to see the strong energies of the previous Spheres become a little milder, made less raw by the civilizing influence of Tiphareth. Netzach is the female quality which sustains nature, so its color is the bright emerald green of leaves and new shoots—this green being formed from the combination of the blue ray of Chesed and the yellow of Tiphareth. No matter what occurs, nature renews itself, gently but surely. The deities of Netzach are usually beautiful goddesses, like the Roman Venus, and the geometrical symbol is the seven-pointed star.

The opposite of this purely sensual Sephirah is the eighth Sphere, called Hod, meaning Splendor. Whereas Netzach is languid and emotional life, Hod is flashing speed and brilliant bolts of lightning. It is the mind, where Netzach is the body. All products of human cunning belong here—business, counting, travel. Its color is orange—red from Geburah and yellow from Tiphareth—and its symbol is the eight-pointed star, composed of two squares set at an angle to each other. The perfect god of Hod is the Roman Mercury. Full of ideas, with wings on his feet, carrying the messages of the gods, Mercury is the patron god of traders, thieves, and all whose life revolves around communication and business.

The ninth Sephirah lies once again on the Middle Pillar, and in conjunction with Netzach and Hod it forms the third triad of the Tree of Life. It is called Yesod and is the Foundation of the Tree. Yesod is a strange Sphere to understand at first, since you would expect the Foundation to be firm and concrete. Yet if it were so, there would be no energy, only stagnation. We are led to believe that our perceived universe surrounding us is fixed and unchanging, but this is not true. So-called solid matter is not at all solid, but composed of endlessly moving and whirling particles. This is the true Foundation—an endless fluid reality that can be shaped at Will—so it is with Yesod. Yesod is the Sphere of the Astral plane, the true reality that lies beneath the illusion of matter. It is the Sphere of the Moon, reflecting the solar light of Tiphareth above it, its symbol the lunar crescent, its color purple, combining the red of Geburah with the blue of Chesed. Yesod is thus the home of all lunar goddesses, from all times and places. The motto of Yesod is one of the greatest mottoes of all magick: Change is Stability.

So we have now seen the three great triads of the Tree. Below all these is one last Sephirah, that of Malkuth, the Kingdom. In Malkuth we find the last repository of all the forces that have moved through the Tree of Life. It is the final daughter of the marriage of Nuit and Hadit that began the entire process of manifestation. Malkuth is our Earth. It, like Da'ath, has no single color—its colors are citrine, olive, russet, and black. These are the colors of the earth, the fields, the plants. Note that it has four colors and its symbol is the cross surrounded by the circle. The goddesses of Malkuth are those deities of olden times that cared for the crops and the land, such as Demeter and Ceres.

As the Middle Pillar forms the trunk of the Tree, Malkuth is its roots buried deep in the earth providing the nourishment which the Tree needs, Yesod the root structure which provides the stability, Tiphareth the body of the trunk from which the branches depend, and Kether its flowering Crown. Take a little time now to visualize once again the entire Tree before you, with all its power coursing through it. Realize that it is a living, growing entity, not just a dead diagram in a book. Although it may be difficult at first, try to learn the shape of the Tree and the colors of the Spheres by heart. See how the gods and goddesses fit with the forces that each Sephirah contains. The easiest and best way to learn the Tree of Life is to paint it for yourself, coloring each Sphere correctly and adding the appropriate symbols to each one. When you have done this, you will have begun to grow your own personal Tree of Life, which will always be there to aid you as you learn.

An excellent habit to adopt is to try to relate everything that happens to you to the Tree of Life. When you go out for a walk, just look around you and try to hang everything you see on one of the branches of your Tree. For example, say you see a postman—to where does he belong? Hod, obviously, he being a messenger, like Mercury. A large guard dog runs up and attacks him—Geburah, violence. You notice that the dog itself is a pit bull terrier, so he may be attributed to Da'ath, which is often called the Pit of Reason. You then see the dog return to the kennel where it sleeps. The kennel is Chesed, foursquare and secure; the sleep is Yesod, ruled by the Moon. See how it works? Practice doing this, and you will begin to perceive links between things that you would have never previously thought of. Keeping this up will literally expand your mind, forging new neural connections in your brain. You might also find it useful to consult Liber 777, which contains several of the correspondences of the Tree of Life laid out in tabular format. You can find the most important sections of it reprinted in *Magick in Theory and Practice*.

Another exercise related to the one before is to sit down at home with a blank Tree of Life diagram and fill in a whole new set of correspondences—try the cast of your favorite film or TV show, for example. You will rarely get the entire cast to fit perfectly onto the Tree, but the attempt can be very illuminating. Let's take one of the all-time greats: *Star Trek*. Everybody knows *Star Trek,* don't they? How does this fit into the Qabalah?

Kether is the Federation, the transcendent unity that all creatures aspire to. Chokmah is the wisdom that directs and informs, so perhaps Mr. Spock would be good here; his twin nature being the reflection of Chokmah as Sphere number 2. Lt. Uhura is attributed to Binah, the Black Mother that receives all transmissions. In Chesed we find Dr. McCoy, the square, conservative countryman who preserves the life of the crew. Geburah is Mr. Sulu, the dashing sword-wielding warrior. Captain Kirk obviously belongs in Tiphareth; he is the shining center about which the crew revolves, full of nobility and energy. Netzach is the enduring force of nature, so here we can put Nurse Chapell whose love for Spock endures no matter what the difficulties, and whose care nourishes all who are sick. In Hod we can place Mr. Chekov, the young cadet scholar who is full of jokes and pranks. The foundation of the whole crew is Mr. Scott, who keeps the ship going through all difficulties. His domain deep in the engine room makes him an obvious candidate for the Yesod attribution. And finally to Malkuth—the Earth—or in this case, the Starship Enterprise itself, which provides the material basis and life support for the work of the crew.

The only thing I'm not sure about is who I can attribute

to Da'ath—perhaps Saavik, the pupil of Spock who appeared in some of the Star Trek movies? After all, she is a "false" member of the crew, and as a half Romulan, not fully of the Federation. Her emphasis on the power of logic is a distinctly Da'athian trait. Oh dear, I seem to be getting carried away here. Anyway I hope you can see from this example how you can use the Tree of Life to order just about everything possible—and have fun while doing it! (How about trying *Star Trek: The Next Generation*? You get more characters to choose from...)

One important thing to understand is that the Tree of Life is not just a symbolic representation of the universe outside you, but also of the universe within you, since each person is a microcosm, a reflection of the whole. When you perform the Banishing Ritual of the Pentagram, for example, you are creating the Tree of Life in your own aura. During the Cross of Light you draw down the force from Kether into Chokmah-Binah in your forehead ("My god is above me"), then down to Yesod in your genitals, across from Geburah on your right shoulder to Chesed on your left, into Tiphareth as you fold your arms upon your chest ("My god is within me"). The next time you perform the pentagram ritual, try visualizing yourself standing within the whole Tree like this. One very good exercise to try is called the Lightning Flash, and I am very grateful to Frater Muladorio for introducing it to me many years ago. This particular version is largely based on ideas given in Liber A'ash, a short Thelemic Holy Book, which you may find useful to read through before you begin. You can find Liber A'ash in Appendix VII of *Magick in Theory and Practice*.

The Lightning Flash

Sit in your asana and ready yourself by performing some basic breathing exercises. When you are prepared, begin to visualize your astral body transformed into a gnarled and blackened oak tree, standing solitary and erect for centuries in the midst of a desolate heath. Imagine your roots stretching far into the earth, drawing water from the depths. Feel your branches stretching up high into the night sky waving in the wind that caresses you. Storm clouds begin to gather above you now, dark, tinged with a blood-red glow. The air gets close, filled with electricity and the roll of thunder drums around you, shaking the ground. Suddenly a searing bolt of lightning erupts from the sky striking your crown, and passing down through you, following the path of energy through your branches (right brain, left brain, throat, right shoulder, left shoulder, chest, right hip, left hip, genitals, base of the spine). The lightning shoots down into the Earth below you, penetrating to its furthest depths, and the Earth's primal volcanic fire surges upward into you. Your roots writhe in ecstasy, and the sap rises upward through your branches, filling you with creative energy until it bursts from the top of the tree into the night sky, becoming a flaming star in Infinite Space. Rest now; then close the exercise in silence by assuming the god-form of Hoor-paar-kraat.

* * *

So far we have dealt only with the Spheres of the Tree—what about all those Paths that connect them? There are twenty-two Paths in total, and each of these Paths also has a force connected with it. Well, more accurately each Path has a complex of forces connected with it, for whereas the Sephiroth are groupings of relatively simple primal powers, the Paths which connect them are much more subtle sets of energies. As such, learning the attributions of these Paths is nowhere near as easy as learning the attributions of the Spheres. Luckily, some very wise Adepts also figured this out many years ago and have given us a very wonderful method of understanding the entire Tree of Life. It is called the tarot.

At the beginning of this book I advised you the reader to get hold of a tarot pack, preferably the edition produced by Aleister Crowley and Lady Frieda Harris. If you have a tarot pack, you should now go get it and spread the cards out in front of you. The pack contains seventy-two cards, divided into three main groups. The first group is of twenty-two cards, numbered from 0 to XXI, called the Trumps, and each one corresponds to a Path of the Tree. Gather together all these Trumps now, and sort them into order. If you have one of the strange packs that contains three cards numbered I, discard two of these Magus cards, so you just have one card of each number. You now hold in your hand a guide to the Paths of the Tree of Life. The Trump cards are attributed to the Paths as shown in the diagram. Note that each Trump also shows on it a Hebrew letter and an astrological sign or something similar.

I do not intend to go into a full explanation of the tarot Trumps and the Paths in this book, for it would take up a great deal too much room and go into too much detail for what is, after all, designed to be a beginner's book. In the next chapter you will learn how to explore these Paths for yourself, so that you can learn, rather than just being taught. In the future, I thoroughly recommend that you get hold of a good book dealing specifically with the tarot and study it closely. Crowley's *Book of Thoth* is by far the best of the bunch, and I cannot even hope to begin to approach its depth.

Of the other cards in the tarot pack, they can be split into two groups. One group is made up of forty cards, divided into four sets of ten each. Sort them out into order, then pick one set. You will see that it is numbered from Ace to 10, and each number corresponds to the appropriate Sphere of the Tree of Life—the Ace corresponds to Kether, the 2 to Chokmah, the 3 to Binah, etc. Note that Da'ath has no card, it being a Sphere with no fixed attributes. Now there are four suits of small cards. Each suit shows a different facet of the Sephiroth of the Tree of Life. The suit of Wands shows the Fire aspect of the Spheres, the suit of Cups shows the Water side, the Swords show the Air side, and the suit of Disks shows the Earth side. For example, the 2 of Cups shows the Water aspect of Chokmah, and thus is called Love, for it is the primary emotional aspect of the Will, or the 6 of Swords is called Science, for science is the harmony of the mental processes. By studying these small cards carefully you can quickly approach a much deeper understanding of the Spheres of the Tree than you would normally be capable of.

The final remaining group of cards are the Court cards, containing sixteen cards divided into four suits, each suit composed of a Knight, Queen, Prince, and Princess. You are already aware that the composition of the suits follows the basic magical convention of Fire, Water, Air, Earth—so do the family relationships of the Court cards. The Knights are attributed to Fire, Queens to Water, Princes to Air, and Princesses to Earth. Thus we have not only elements, but sub-elements. Let's take the Cups "family" as an example. The Queen of Cups is attributed to Water of Water—in the material world this could be, for example, the sea. Prince of Cups is Air of Water, which could describe clouds, water in gaseous form, and Princess of Cups is Earth of Water, which can be symbolized by ice, water in solid form. Knight of Cups is Fire of Water—this could be steam, water in its hottest form—or perhaps alcohol might be even more fitting.

The Court cards can also be fitted onto the Tree of Life in another manner, known as the Four Worlds of the Qabalah. The Four Worlds are: Atziluth, the Archetypal World; Briah, the Creative World; Yetzirah, the Formative World; and Assiah, the Material World. For our purposes we can consider Atziluth to be similar to Chokmah and corresponding to the Knight. Briah is Binah and corresponds to the Queen. Yetzirah is composed of all the Sephiroth from Da'ath to Yesod, forming a hexagram with Tiphareth at its center, and attributed to the Prince. The last of the Four Worlds is Assiah, which is in Malkuth, and corresponds to the Princess. At first sight it may seem that these Four Worlds are an unnecessary complication to the system, but they can be a useful concept in certain situations, so keep them in mind.

**

One very good way of really getting to grips with the Qabalah is through divination. Since the Tree of Life is a map which is capable of containing all possibilities, then theoretically one should be able to find the answer to any problem within its borders. So by using the Tarot cards we can build patterns of energy lines which we can use to attain a deeper perception of reality. There are many different methods of reading the tarot—I recommend this method, called the hexagram spread.

The hexagram spread is based on the Qabalistic World of Yetzirah, the Formative World, and consists of thirteen cards—one card in the central position surrounded by six pairs of cards. The procedure is as follows. First take the entire pack of seventy-two cards in your left hand, and sit quietly for a moment stilling your mind. With your right hand (or magick wand) draw a hexagram in the air over the cards, saying:

I invoke thee, great Tahuti, whose Wisdom has created these cards; guide me in my quest for Understanding.

Visualize your question clearly and begin to shuffle the cards thoroughly. Now deal out the cards in the following order:

Place the first card in the central position (Tiphareth, the Sun). The second card goes below this, in the place of Yesod, the Moon. Third, top left, in the position of Geburah, Mars. Fourth, top right, Chesed, Jupiter. (These last three cards form a downward-pointing triangle.) Fifth, below Chesed, place a card in the position of Netzach, Venus. Sixth, bottom left, Hod, Mercury. Seventh, right at the top, Da'ath, Saturn. Now repeat the process, putting a second card beside each one already laid out except for the central solar card which remains alone. You will have dealt out thirteen cards in total, exactly one-sixth of the total pack.

The central card is in the place of the Sun and represents the situation that you now find yourself in. The six paired cards can be divided into two main groups—a downward-pointing triangle formed by the cards in the places of Yesod, Geburah, and Chesed; and an upward-pointing triangle formed by the cards in the places of Netzach, Hod, and Da'ath. The downward-pointing triangle represents the forces at work in this situation; the upward-pointing triangle represents the possible outcome in the future.

Starting with the downward triangle: the cards in the place of Yesod, the Moon, tell you your unconscious motivations. The cards in the place of Geburah show your conscious desires. The pair of cards in the place of Chesed show the outside environmental influences that are affecting the problem.

The upward triangle: the cards occupying the place of Netzach show the likeliest resolution of the situation if you were to take no action to change things. The cards in Hod, the Sphere of Mercury, advise you on a particular course of action that you may take. And the cards at the top of the figure, in the place of Saturn, show what will occur if you do act on the advice given.

Note that in each of the outside positions there are two cards. This makes the spread a little bit more difficult to read than some other tarot spreads, but has the advantage of showing a lot more subtlety. The pairs of cards work together, so when you are attempting to read the spread, try to work out just what meaning a particular combination of cards can have.

Divination is useful in two different ways. One, it can help you see things that are happening around you that you might sometimes miss and gives you suggestions on what to do about it. Two, it can really help you learn how to use the Qabalah as a dynamic living system to help you order your thoughts and feelings. Although in some ways divination may seem preposterous, at the end of the day it works and works extraordinarily well. Keep it as a valuable item in your magician's toolbox.

Note for experienced students: I have emphasized throughout this chapter the three-dimensional aspect of the Tree of Life although for convenience we normally draw it on a two-dimensional piece of paper. Unfortunately many occult authors do not seem to be aware of this and in their books have assumed that the Tree is a two-dimensional figure, with the Sephiroth being shaped like flat coins, not as Spheres. This misunderstanding has sometimes given rise to speculation that there might be a "backside of the Tree," complete with totally different attributions of the Sephiroth and Paths. Although this may be an interesting intellectual exercise with which to while away an idle winter's evening, it is of little value magically.

Further Study

Magick—Part III, Chapter 0: The Magical Theory of the Universe
Magick—Appendix V
Magick—Appendix VII: Liber A'ash vel Capricorni Pneumatici
Magick Without Tears—Introduction: Letter F
Magick Without Tears—Chapter 4: The Qabalah: The Best Training for Memory

CHAPTER TEN

ASTRAL TRAVELING

What is reality? There we have the proverbial 64,000 dollar question. Answer: I don't know, and neither do you, otherwise you wouldn't be wasting your time reading this attempt to explain it. One thing we do know, however, is that all we know of reality is what we perceive and our perceptions are limited. This is easy to prove—can you see the moons of Saturn from where you are sitting now? I assume the answer is no. Yet those moons exist and are huge. However your eyesight is limited, so you cannot see them. All you can see is all you can see. You can never know the fullest extent of reality by using your sense organs. All you can know is all you can perceive. In other words, your entire universe is a product of your perception. And since your perception is but a part of your mental faculties, your entire universe exists inside your head.

There are two, and only two, possible views of reality. Either there is something out there beyond our minds or there isn't. We can never know the answer to this question, since all our perceptions take place within our minds. From a practical point of view, it really doesn't matter whether an external reality exists or not, since ultimately we act as if we know it does exist, even though we can only know our own internal reality.

If all reality lies inside the mind, then how can we ultimately decide which things are a product of our minds, and which have an objective existence outside it? The answer to this is simple. We can't. We can never know which things are more "real" than others, since there is no absolute test we can give. Frankly, this can be a pain in the ass to magicians, who need to understand reality in order to function more efficiently within it.

Yes, I know that this is supposed to be a meditation chapter, not a philosophy one, but in these last chapters the lines between theory and practice are going to become increasingly blurred as we delve deeper into the uses of magical energy. What I'm leading up to here is an important point, one that I have touched on in previous chapters: *reality is a point of view*. Our minds being the complicated things that they are, this implies that our reality is also at least as complex. On top of that, our minds being the changeable things they are implies that our reality is in a continual state of flux. Reality cannot be a steady state. As our minds change, reality changes. As our perception grows, so does the universe, since our universe comes from our perception. Every time you sit down on your ass to meditate, you change the world. Hopefully you're making it a more fun place to be in!

So we have seen that reality is flexible. If that's so, why doesn't this chair I am sitting on sprout wings and fly me away to the moons of Saturn? Good question. Let's just say that one thing reality seems to need is coherence, that is, a set of rules that establish how reality holds itself together. It may well be that the external reality (if indeed there is such a thing) has no rules, is pure chaos, but our perception certainly needs rules in order to function properly, so rules we have.

One seeming exception to all this is the dream reality. I call this a reality too, for it happens in our heads and affects us deeply—and it is totally real to us while we are in it. Yet in a dream the normal laws of the universe seem to go out the window. Like I say, reality is flexible. At the same time, you have probably noticed that dreams have their own logic to them. Although very strange things happen, while you dream you operate within the parameters of the dream world's laws, and these strange happenings do not seem strange at all. It is only upon awakening that you perceive their strangeness. If, as sometimes happens during a dream, something occurs that does not fit the reality that the dream has built up, it stands out of the dream like an out of tune instrument in a symphony orchestra. This can often be so obtrusive that it wakes you up out of the dream, since your mind does not wish to accept what seems to be a noncoherent reality.

So now we have an idea of why my chair can sprout wings and fly in a dream, but not in "normal" consciousness. It has to do with the laws of the particular reality that we're dealing with. In most people's "normal" reality, a chair cannot fly, but in some of their dream realities it can. It is simply a matter of coherence, of the logic of the particular world that we are living in at the time. The laws of most people's "normal" reality seem to be fairly rigid, whereas the laws of some other realities are plastic and make it easy to mold that reality into different shapes. Note that I have begun here to talk about realities in the plural. A dream is real, that you know if you've ever woken up sweating in terror from a nightmare or woken up wildly physically aroused from a deep sexual fantasy. If it can affect your body that much, it's *real*. And if it's real, but different from our normal reality, then we can assume that it is another form of reality, effectively another reality completely. We inhabit multiple realities; we shift from one to another frequently. Remember that reality is a point of view!

There is one further point about our experiences in these multiple realities that we may inhabit. Each experience that we have affects the way that we perceive other things in the future. Where our perception is thus changed, it is changed forever and for all realities. If you did the blindfold experiment I suggested in chapter 7 (and if you haven't please do it soon), you will know what I am talking about here. All the familiar objects around you suddenly became strange and alien while you were in the blindfolded state—but even when you had taken off the blindfold again, your perception of those previously familiar objects was no longer the same. They looked different and felt different. So your experience of one reality, the "blind" reality, has changed another reality, the "seeing" reality. In other words, any change that takes place in one reality changes forever all other realities—since all realities are experienced through your perception, every time your perception changes, *all* realities change.

The discoveries of the preceding paragraphs form the theoretical basis of a whole system of magick. It can be summed up in three theorems:

I: Reality is multiple and flexible, but always coherent.
A: Some realities are more flexible than others.
O: Any change in one reality brings a corresponding change in all realities.

Can you see from this how our magick can work? Since we are living in a world where the physical laws seem rigid and unyielding, if we want to change something, we can do so more easily by journeying to another world where the laws are more flexible and conducive to our Will and effecting our change there. Then when we return to this world, we will find that a corresponding change has also taken place here.

Notice that I talk about a corresponding change. This does not mean that the change brought about in one reality will necessarily be exactly the same as the change brought about in another, only that the changes are related. Since the laws of each universe are different, the changes that happen in those universes must also be somehow different. However, since the changes are brought about primarily by changing our perception, and we use the same senses in all realities, then these changes, although slightly different, must be of a similar type, no matter what reality we go to.

In order to make this magick effective, we need some way of checking how things in one reality correspond to those in other realities. This is where the Qabalah becomes invaluable, since the Qabalah is a system that shows the relationship between all things. With the Qabalah as your guide, you can safely step out into any reality, no matter how fluid, safe in the assurance that you have a map to show you the way. There are a huge collection of flexible realities, and for just about all of them the Qabalah can be used to steer a course to your destination.

Magicians call this collection of very flexible realities the astral plane. The astral plane is similar in many ways to dream realities, or fantasy realities. It is a group of environments containing just about anything that our minds are capable of imagining, and our minds are certainly capable of imagining a lot! One thing is for sure: there is no human being who lacks imagination, no matter how dull they may seem on the surface. The imagination itself is our mode of transport to the astral realms; it is the key that unlocks the doors between worlds.

So how do we operate in these worlds, these alternate realities? If they are all so different, so bizarre, each with different laws, how do we know what to do once we get there? This is where being a Thelemic magician really helps. There is one law, and one only, that seems to cut a diagonal slash across all parts of the astral plane: the Law of Thelema. Do what thou wilt shall be the whole of the Law. Thelema provides the constant basis that all realities depend on. I say constant, but I do not mean stable. The Law of Thelema itself is dynamic, indeed must be, in order to remain workable across all the shifts that these realities go through. In the astral plane, change is the only constant.

Non-Thelemic magicians on the astral plane usually have a big problem. Their magical system postulates a certain set of fixed rules and laws which their reality should obey. This limits their capacity to freely move through truly flexible spaces, since all that they can comprehend are those things that can fit into their laws. Anything that they come across which does not fit into their limited worldview cannot be understood by them. As Thelemites, we can accept and comprehend all things and all beings, since they must conform to the destiny of their own Will. If they go against their own Wills, they weaken their own position within the reality they inhabit, since they go against the most fundamental law underlying all realities.

I think that that is enough theory for now—your head is probably spinning trying to fully comprehend the last few paragraphs. I know mine is. Don't worry if you don't fully understand what I'm getting at. As with everything else in this book, the best way to learn is to put the theory into practice. That's what we'll do in next section.

Let's explode one myth for a start—that experiencing different realities is hard. It's not. You do it all the time. Dreaming is a perfect example of this, but it does have the problem that normally on the dream plane you have no control over your Will. The states of mind brought about by hallucinogenic drugs are another good example, and if you've tried these substances, you'll need no persuasion from me about their effectiveness. Again though, keeping track of the Will can be difficult, especially if the drugs are addictive.

Please note: I do not recommend the use of any hallucinogenic drugs in achieving altered states of awareness, unless you are willing and capable of following recommended procedures. These include, but are not limited to:

A good knowledge of the chemical composition of the substance you are ingesting; a good knowledge of its history and the culture surrounding its use; a working knowledge of basic traditional shamanic techniques; an appropriate setting for the working you wish to perform; a "control," or guide person, who also is aware of all of these procedures and who is sufficiently experienced to remain in full control of all mental and physical faculties; the telephone number of the nearest emergency hospital. Oh, and sell all of your Carlos Castaneda books beforehand as well. In fact, don't trust any advice that emanated from the sixties. You don't want to end up like your parents.

The easiest way to start to experience other realities is to go back to the most common one—dream reality. The peculiar laws of the dream worlds make them some of the most fluid of all realities, the major drawback being that they are so difficult to control. If we can find a way to exert that control, we're getting somewhere. This essentially means that we will have to learn how to "wake up," while still dreaming. There are several techniques for achieving this.

The first thing you will have to do is keep your Magical Diary by your bedside, along with a pen. When you wake up in the morning (or the afternoon if you're like some magicians I know!), the absolute first thing you must do is to write down all your memories of your dreams of the night. If you have a bed partner, it can also be helpful to tell them everything right away. This can be embarrassing, but also very therapeutic. In the beginning, remembering can be difficult, but every day that you do this it becomes a little easier, until after a few weeks or so you will begin to remember much more vividly. After you have written down your dreams, you can try analyzing them with the Qabalah to see which things might correspond to things in your waking reality.

Not only will you remember your dreams much more vividly, the dreams themselves will often become much more vivid and charged with symbolism. This shows that already your mind is reaching deeper down into this strange new world. Now it is time to begin to wake up in your dream. This process is called lucid dreaming. The technique essentially consists of implanting a trigger mechanism in your mind which will act like a sort of alarm clock for the dream world. This trigger can be any object at all, but should be something that you can be sure that you will encounter in your travels through the dream plane. Your own hands make an excellent trigger. Every night, before you go to sleep, hold your hands out in front of you and stare deeply at them for a few minutes. Repeat the words: "Wake up, wake up!" as a mantra while you do this. Then as you lie in bed, close your eyes and again visualize your hands in front of you, and silently repeat "Wake up, wake up!" until you fall asleep. Now when you dream, there will be a very good chance that you will see your hands at some point during the dream, and the mantra will immediately come back into your head. At this moment there is a strong possibility that your awareness of yourself will come flooding back to you, and you will be effectively awake while still within the dream world. Now the fun starts. You can do almost anything you want, and the dream world will accommodate you. My favorite trick is to fly, which is so goddamn wonderful I wish that I could do it all the time (without an airplane that is).

OK, I have to admit that it's not quite as easy as I may have made it out to be. It can take some people a very long time to achieve even one lucid dream, and it never becomes something that you can perform night after night, but it's worth the effort considering the fun you can have. Even if you don't manage it at all at first, don't worry, it's really not so important, except as a step to the next phase, which is true waking astral travel.

What you need to do now is to find a way to move onto the astral plane at any time, with full control and awareness. The easiest way is through guided meditation, or pathworking as it is often called. The following section is a pathworking which takes you through the building of your own astral temple, called the Temple of Thelema. This temple is a very useful construct, as it gives you the facility of being able to do full magical rituals at any time, no matter whether you have the right surroundings and equipment with you or not. All the equipment you need for your magick can be created in an astral form and stored in the Temple. The idea of building a temple in another reality may seem strange to you at first, but it shouldn't be. After all, people build temples in this reality, and this reality is harder to work with than most.

The best way to do this pathworking is to find a sympathetic partner who will read it out to you. They should read very slowly and carefully, pausing after every sentence so that you have time to visualize all that is being described. If you cannot find a friend to do this, you can do almost as well by first recording yourself reading the passage on a tape recorder and then playing the tape back later when you want to perform the exercise. For best results, you should set up your room well beforehand. Light the room with only one candle, enough to see the text by, burn some incense (a combination of jasmine and rose joss sticks are ideal for this purpose), and wear your robe and sit in your asana. It's also a good idea to perform a banishing ritual of the pentagram both before and after the exercise.

THE TEMPLE OF THELEMA

The Temple has four square walls made of lapis lazuli and jasper; the floor is alternating squares of silver and gold. A scent of jasmine and rose is in the air. You are sitting in the form of Hoor-paar-kraat in the center of a large circle of green, a single candle lighting each of the cardinal points. Inside the circumference of the circle are inscribed the words: THERION, HADIT, BABALON, NUIT, in red letters. Directly below your feet is marked the Tau cross of ten squares, and before you and behind you to each side are diamonds which form the outline of a triangle within the circle.

In the center of each wall of the temple is a gate, or doorway. You have entered through none of these, but through a secret door given solely unto you, for this is your holy place, a place which has been untouched throughout the centuries.

In front of you is the altar, in the East of the Temple. It is formed by two cubes placed one on top of the other, made of brass, and upon it are a small cross, a single rose, and the Stele of Revealing. The Stele glows softly for it radiates the magick of the Aeon.

Beyond the altar, the god Ra-Hoor-Khuit is enthroned. He is tall, forceful, with a hawk's head, and carries in his right hand the Double Wand of Power, the Wand of the Force of Coph Nia, though his left hand is empty. You now salute him with the words of the law, standing in the sign of the Enterer:

Do what thou wilt shall be the whole of the Law.
Love is the law, love under will.

Strength and light radiate from the god, and assuming the sign of Silence, you feel joy and beauty arise and fill you.

Now you raise your eyes above him. There is no ceiling to the Temple, only the night-blue sky, spangled with the light, faint and faery, of the stars.

You chant the invocation from the Stele of Revealing:

A ka dua
Tuf ur biu
Bi a'a chefu
Dudu ner af a nuteru

From the skies the Priestess appears, bathed in moonlight, her eyes burning, naked but for a sword girt about her waist. She calls forth the flame of your heart on her love-chant:

To Me! To Me!

You may lie a little in her bosom, but slowly she withdraws and is concealed.

The ritual now is ended, with the word:

ABRAHADABRA

You feel yourself sink down through the floor and back into your body on the Earth below.

NOTES ON THE TEMPLE OF THELEMA

Lapis lazuli is a turquoise-blue stone, jasper a dark green stone.

The Tau cross of ten squares is another form of the Tree of Life. It is shaped like an inverted T, with six squares running vertical and five horizontal. The vertical squares represent Kether (top), Chokmah, Binah, Tiphareth, Yesod, and

Malkuth (bottom). The horizontal squares represent Geburah (far left), Hod, Malkuth, Netzach, and Chesed (far right).

* * *

This is the basis of your pathworking technique. Now that you have visited the Temple for the first time, it is always available for your personal use. After you have gone through the pathworking a few times, you should find that you can remember all the things that should be there and that they begin to assume an independent existence. Most important, you will find that the figures of the god and the Priestess are really living entities, and you can talk to them, ask for their advice and assistance. This can be a very useful way of learning more about magick for yourself. You can also try to walk around a bit and see the Temple from different angles (or fly around in your asana if you prefer—I often do this). When you are sure that you have familiarized yourself with the layout of the Temple and you feel confident about being there, you can try exploring further. Remember the four doors? They lead out to various regions of the astral plane. The gate in front of you normally leads to the regions corresponding to the element of Earth, to your left is Air, behind you in the South of the Temple is Water, and to the right is the gate of Fire. These are of course only rough working attributions; these doorways can lead you to anywhere you choose.

The way to use the doors is this. Figure out which region of the astral you wish to explore. Let's say you want to visit the Fire region. When you are in the Temple of Thelema, turn to your right and go over to the door there. On the door at eye level visualize the tattwa symbol of Fire, the red triangle. Concentrate deeply on this symbol. Holding it in your mind, pass through the gate and into the realm beyond. You will find yourself in a whole new landscape, where all that inhabits it are things of Fire. You will see many strange things here, but always keep your Qabalistic learning at the front of your mind. For example, if you are in the Fire realm, you will not expect to see a fresh stream of cool water, so if this appears, you can be sure that you have taken a wrong turn somewhere or that something is playing tricks on you.

You will also frequently meet with creatures that live in these realms. Every time you meet one, you should examine it closely and challenge it. By this I mean that you should check to ensure that the creature is what it appears to be, for sometimes these elementals like to try to disguise their true natures from you. The best way to challenge them is to greet them with the words of the Law of Thelema and/or with appropriate Words of Power, such as ABRAHADABRA. If they reply properly, you can feel relatively sure that they're OK. Check their appearance and clothing. Do they correspond with the realm that you are in? If you are in the Fire realm, a gentle entity wearing light blue flowing robes is going to look as out of place as a schoolmistress in a wrestling ring. If they are wrong, make a banishing pentagram before them, and bid them show their true form or return to the realm from whence they came. Don't forget this, as it is most important that you do not allow any astral entities or objects to appear where they should not be. If you are still having problems, assume the god-form of Hoor-paar-kraat to build up your defenses or the god-form of Ra-Hoor-Khuit if you want to do some serious strong-arm stuff. Remember that Ra-Hoor-Khuit is nearby in the Temple of Thelema, and he will come to your assistance if you call upon him. If you really get into trouble, bolt for the safety of the Temple. Nothing can harm you in there, no matter how freaky it may be. I actually once saw a demon try to invade the Temple of Thelema. He lived just long enough to really regret it before being fried to a crisp.

You will find that these entities have strong personalities, and you can build up good relationships with some of them. You can also learn much about their realms by talking to them or asking them to guide you around. You should ask them to give you their names, for from their names you can tell a good deal about them, and you can call on them again on later trips. Always be courteous to them, for you are a guest in their home, but never allow them to take advantage of you or to demand things from you. And above all, never believe blindly what they tell you, but always check it by whatever means you have at your disposal. If you do believe everything you're told, you will quickly get a reputation as gullible, and next time you enter the astral every idiot demon will be trying to trick you. Above all, these demons love to flatter your ego, so if (when!) one comes along and tells you that you are the chosen teacher of light for the new age of mankind, kindly kick its ass and tell it to leave you alone or you'll cut it into little pieces with your magick sword.

Note that you can create astral weapons just as easily as you can create an astral temple. The best thing is to use the astral forms of the weapons that you already possess on this plane, since they have a strong connection to you already, but there is no need to stick solely to these. You can build special magical instruments for use on particular planes, and you can store them in the Temple of Thelema, where they will always be ready for use when you need them. One magician friend of mine who enjoyed venturing into rather dark and hostile astral regions decided that a magick sword just didn't pack enough firepower, so he designed an astral assault rifle to replace it. He assures me that it does the job very well indeed.

Don't forget that when you are finished with your journeying, you should retrace your steps back to the Temple of Thelema. Don't worry about getting lost; this is impossible, for you always retain a link to your point of entry to the astral. Just concentrate your Will, and you will find yourself rapidly drawn back to the Temple. Once there, salute Ra-Hoor-Khuit again, go back to your asana, and sink back down through the floor into your material body.

You can explore the worlds appropriate to almost any element, planet, idea, or symbol. After you have tried the tattwa symbols, you might like to try exploring tarot cards. You can explore the minor cards by painting the number of the card on one of the Temple doorways. For example, to explore the two of Cups card, simply go the Western door of the Temple of Thelema, because this is the door that corresponds to the element Water and to the tarot suit of Cups. Draw a large number 2 in light on the doorway, just like you normally draw a pentagram when you're doing the pentagram ritual. You can also recite the name of the appropriate Sphere of the Tree of Life as a mantra perhaps—Chokmah in this case. Then walk through the doorway into the world of this card. If you wish to find out about one of the court cards, you could try drawing a crown on the door, and perhaps you might find yourself in the royal court when you go through the door (just like Alice did when she went through the Looking Glass). If you want to explore the Trump cards, it's slightly more difficult since these cards represent very complex energies, not primal elemental forces like the other cards. Perhaps it's best to visualize the card as a special doorway appearing right in front of you in the center of the Temple or above you, filling the sky above the Temple, and then fly up into it. Try it and see what works for you.

You can also use Yi Jing (I Ching) hexagrams as doorways or geometrical figures or indeed any symbol that you wish to find out more about. One good tip when using a symbol like this is to draw it out beforehand, to make it easier to memorize. If you draw it on a small square of paper or card, you can use it in the ritual. At the beginning of the meditation, you should anoint the symbol with holy oil. Oil of Abramelin is ideal for this purpose, but if you can't find it, almost any essential oil will do. Then anoint yourself with the oil, drawing a small cross and circle on your forehead, just above the eyebrows. Pick up the paper with the symbol on it and press it to your forehead. The oil should make it stick in place. Now continue with the Temple of Thelema exercise as usual. You should find that your entry into the plane of the symbol is greatly enhanced. You can also use a mantra appropriate to the plane you wish to visit if you want; some people find that this is also helpful.

For those who wish to explore the paths of the Tree of

Life in depth, I also highly recommend using a method based on Liber 231, published in *The Holy Books of Thelema*. This short document gives the sigils and names of various guardian angels that serve to guide Thelemic magicians on their astral journeys. There are two angels for each path, one representing its positive aspects, the other representing its negative ones. Or in other words, one representing the path as it is seen from the bottom going up, the other from the top down. If this confuses you, just think about when you go on a journey somewhere. The way back is the same as the way there, but it often looks and feels totally different.

The way to use Liber 231 is similar to what I have already described. Draw the sigil of the Angel that you wish to invoke on a small piece of parchment, card, or paper. Memorize the Angel's name, do your banishing rite, etc., then anoint the sigil and stick it to your forehead. Repeat the Angel's name as a mantra, at the same time visualizing the sigil that you have drawn. You will find yourself drawn to an astral landscape, and if you keep calling the name, the Angel will appear and guide you through the region. I have done this several times, and I have found that these Angels are the most helpful and useful I have encountered anywhere. I highly recommend this exercise for those who are serious about astral travel. Don't forget to send the Angels my greetings when you meet them!

Note that in Liber 231 the Angels are referred to as Genii, which has led some people to speculate that they are somehow connected with Aladdin's lamp. Not so, the word "Genii" here is the plural form of the Latin word *Genius*, meaning a Guardian Angel (yes, this is the origin of our word "genius"—interesting, no?).

The last point I need to make here is that above all be sure to bring your consciousness fully back to this plane of existence when you are finished with your brief journey to an alternate reality. When you come back to your body, clap your hands together hard eleven times in a 3-5-3 rhythm, then stand up and stamp your feet eleven times on the ground. Make sure that you clap hard enough so that you can feel your hands sting—there's nothing like a little pain to make you completely aware of your body (as you found out doing Liber Jugorum ...). Although astral worlds can be fascinating things, always remember that there's no place like home...

FURTHER STUDY

Magick—Chapter 18
Magick—Appendix III
Magick Without Tears—Chapter 17: Astral Journey

CHAPTER ELEVEN

MAGICK POWER

So far in your training, the magick you have been performing has been a fairly introverted affair. This has been intentional on my part, as I do think that this encourages you to keep examining yourself at every step and to work at a pace which is most effective for you. But I must confess that I personally, being the extrovert that I am, do like to get up and do some serious rock 'n' roll magick as frequently as I can. What we're going to get to grips with now is the raising of magical power. You already have all the basic structures for doing magick; now we will concentrate on energizing those structures.

Until now, most of your magick has been static, performed either while you have been motionless in asana or when your movement has consisted of just walking around in a circle. But you should already know from your yoga practice just how much your bodily state can influence your magical abilities. Through yoga we silence all the body's activities so that they do not distract us from our magical intent. This is like the process of performing a banishing ritual—it gets rid of all influences that may act on us. Magical movement, on the other hand, is like the process of invocation—it calls only the specific energies we require down into our bodies.

One of the greatest problems in writing about body techniques is that most of you who are reading this book have been brought up in a society which surrounds the functions of the body with taboos. For some this can mean that they have great problems in releasing body energies in a natural manner. Leading a Thelemic lifestyle can help greatly, which is why the Thelemic morality described in chapter 6 is an important prerequisite to many of the exercises that will be described in this chapter.

Just about the oldest and most common technique for raising magical energy is dancing. Music and dance do not play a large part in most Thelemic writings, mainly because Aleister Crowley, by his own admission, had a tin ear when it came to music. I, on the other hand, must admit to bias in this matter since I am (in my other life) a professional musician and record producer. Be that as it may, integrating music and dance into your rituals is highly recommended.

If you have had no experience in dance before, there are two types that I recommend you try. One is very primitive shamanic music, which depends for its effect on strong rhythms and repeated chanting; the other is very modern electronic club music. These musics are closely related magically, in that they have as their primary function the creation of trance states. They differ greatly from most other music which is primarily designed for either pure entertainment or to transmit a particular intellectual message. There is nothing wrong with entertainment or intelligence, but in this context we are looking for magical tools. You have probably already heard examples of these types of music, but hearing is not enough. To be valid as magical tools, trance music must be experienced through the entire body. Please note that when I talk of trance music, I absolutely do not mean meandering, drifting "New Age" music. Regardless of its validity as an artistic concept, in my opinion this sort of stuff is the antithesis of what we need in our magick. I have lost count of the number of rituals I have participated in where there was some bland burbling nonsense coming from a ghetto blaster in the corner, serving only to take the edge off any power that was coming through.

Practical advice: if you haven't done so already, try to find an all-night rave in your neighborhood, go there in some loose clothing, and spend at least one continuous hour dancing. Don't worry if you think you're too fat, old, or horrendously ugly, I guarantee very few people will be paying any attention (most of them will be too stoned to care ...). Don't worry about whether you actually like the music or not; that really doesn't matter—it's not entertainment we're interested in here, it's achieving a trance state. While you dance, try integrating other magical techniques, like reciting a mantra. It is also good to simply focus your eyes on a flashing light and let yourself be drawn into that light, while you invoke a particular god or goddess. I have done all this many times, and it remains one of my favorite ways of performing magick (it can also get you laid if you're lucky ...). Under no circumstances, however, should you try focusing your attention on a strobe light—they're the white ones that blink on and off very brightly and rapidly. A friend of mine tried this once and ended up writhing on the floor in an epileptic fit—not recommended.

If you've danced at raves before, you will probably have noticed an unusual phenomenon. As you dance, you seem to be able to feel something of the moods of the people around you. This brings us to a very important point: that magical energy can be shared by a group of people. All of the exercises given so far have assumed that you have been working solo, but being alone with your magick all the time is not usually an ideal situation. Sooner or later, you should attempt to work with other magicians. The biggest problem is finding some ...

You may already know one or two other people with the same interests as you, and if so, you shouldn't have any real problems working together, as long as you ensure that your magical interests and your personal relationships do not begin to conflict. I can almost guarantee that eventually they will. Magick puts great stress on the mental and physical faculties, and this can cause big problems between people who work together. I can only recommend most highly that you always keep Thelemic principles in mind when these stress situations arise; otherwise you are probably going to end up in deep shit, frankly speaking.

It can also be a good idea to get in touch with a working magical Order. There are many of these, of varying quality and capacity; some are small local bodies, others are large international groups. The foremost Thelemic Order is the Ordo Templi Orientis, of which I myself have been an initiate for many years. I highly recommend that if you wish to follow the Thelemic path, you consider joining the OTO. The OTO system contains within it one of the most important sources of magical energy—the initiation. To be initiated means to be permanently united to a current of magical energy that is already flowing. In a sense, by doing the exercises in this book you have already started on the process of initiation as a Thelemic magician. You may already have been able to perceive the Thelemic current flowing through you as you work. By going through full initiation into a genuine magical Order, that energy is fully activated within your psyche.

* * *

There are many other ways to increase the energy level generated in your magick. Another traditional method is through fasting. If you deny your physical body food, your entire astral makeup begins to change, and your magical energies change rapidly. You have to be careful with this, however, since obviously going without food can be harmful to your health and is ultimately fatal in most cases.

Before you perform any major magical working, fasting for at least four hours is a good idea, especially if the working you intend to perform is a Mass (I'll describe what this is later in the chapter). You should drink plenty of water or herbal tea while you are fasting; this will help clear out toxins from the body. Do not drink tap water if you can help it; mineral water is much better. Many magicians will fast for a whole weekend sometimes if they have something really special to do. If you want to try this, *be careful!* I recommend that you make sure that you have someone around most of the time and are not too stressed or under psychological pressure at the time. I say this because on a magical fast you can easily drift off into astral wanderings and have trouble getting your feet back on the ground. Every time I fast I get really dreamy but also really energetic, and I find my magical power massively increased. But it does affect my psyche deeply. Be aware of this. If you're fasting and at any time feel that you are not totally in control of the process, gently break your fast and slowly bring yourself back to normal consciousness. Oh, when you do break your fast, do not gobble loads of food; it might make you sick.

A technique that is often associated with fasting is flagellation—yes, that does mean whipping. Being whipped or otherwise put into pain does some very interesting things to one's mind as well as one's body. The most important thing for our purposes is that pain causes the body to release endorphins, the body's natural painkiller, and these endorphins can be used to alter your consciousness. Whipping is one of the best ways to do this, since it can release enormous amounts of endorphins without permanently damaging the body.

If you're working alone, you can easily flagellate yourself with a cat-o'-nine tails type of whip. This is consists of a firm handle, made of wood or something similar, attached to various strips of flexible leather. Take off your shirt, hold the whip handle, and throw the leather section over your shoulder so that the strips hit your back. You'll feel a mild sting. Keep doing this, preferably while reciting a mantra and concentrating on the goddess or god that you want to invoke. To begin with, don't hit yourself too hard. It doesn't actually have to hurt much for you to feel the effect. Just concentrate on keeping the rhythm of your breathing, your mantra, and your whipping in synchronization. Eventually you'll start to feel yourself getting into a slightly altered state. Don't go too far the first couple of times—it is easy to physically damage yourself if you get into a trance too quickly. With practice you'll begin to sense what your limits are.

I realize that some of you are reading this and thinking: "Is this guy crazy? Whipping? This is weird."—especially since most of you probably associate whipping with either punishment or sexual stimulation. Be wary of letting magical flagellation turn into either of these things unless you are really confident that you know what you're doing. This is especially important if you are engaging in the practice with someone else.

Which brings us to sex. You've been waiting for this bit, haven't you? Maybe you've even skipped on here while flicking through the book hoping to find something juicy. I know that's what I do when I see a book in the shop with "Sex Magick" on the cover ...

Sex magick is undoubtedly a very powerful (and fun!) technique, but I earnestly warn all the readers of this book against it. That surprised you, didn't it? This book is for beginners, and beginners should definitely not try sex magick in my opinion. It is too dangerous for themselves and for others. It is also quite difficult to do properly, given that most people in a state of sexual excitement tend to think with their genitals rather than their brains (especially men, if I can be forgiven for being sexist here). However since sex is an important technique, I'll drop you some hints.

The first thing to understand is that if you want to do sex magick you should be proficient in all the yoga techniques that I have given in this book so far. If you're not, and you start using sex in your workings, you're heading for a whole mess of trouble. You need the strength of body and mind that yoga gives you if you are to have any long-term success.

The second thing is that you should be endeavoring to follow the Thelemic way of life as expressed in Liber OZ (see chapter 6). If you don't do this, the morality that has been programmed into you from childhood will cause you big problems. Now I can hear people reading this saying: "I don't have any problem with morality ..." If so, I'd like to meet you. I've been around and met lots of people who told me this. I'd say half of them knew they were lying; the other half were lying too and just didn't know it.

So make sure that you heed my words before you get your pants off. If you don't, I'll expect a letter of apology from you in six months saying that I was right and you wish you'd listened to me in the first place.

So what's so good about sex magick? There are several

answers to this. The most obvious one is that sexuality and magical energy are closely related, just as sexuality and creativity are closely related. Increase your sexual energy and you will increase your potential magical energy.

Your first sexual magick experiments should be alone. If someone else is around, you'll increase any chance of embarrassment you might suffer from, and you'll find it much, much harder to concentrate. Even if you're in the closest marriage in the entire history of the world, I advise that you keep this secret from your partner until you've tried it a couple of times and feel reasonably confident. The main reason for this is to ensure that the morality issue is kept as far away as possible.

So figure out what you want to invoke, do a banishing rite, then start your mantra and visualization as normal. While you do so, start to masturbate slowly. Do not concern yourself over the reaction of the body. Concentrate on the purpose of the working. If at any time you begin to get more involved in the sex than the magick (if you get my drift), stop masturbating and calm yourself until your concentration is OK again. I recommend that at first you do not allow yourself to attain orgasm, although the temptation may be strong! Simply let your excitement subside of its own accord while you complete the ritual. Remember to banish thoroughly! Write down every detail of what you did and felt in your Diary. If you are still feeling horny (you probably will be), you can bring yourself to an orgasm *afterwards*—perhaps this time it's better if you have help doing that ...

After you've tried this a few times, you can start allowing yourself to get to orgasm—but don't lose your concentration! Don't kid yourself, this is difficult. You'll find that this sort of magick is very powerful indeed, but please, please, please be careful and *take your time*. Don't try to become the world's greatest magician and lover overnight. This sort of thing takes years, if not decades, to master.

I'm not going to go into more detail here, because it's outside the scope of this book. Sorry. You're on your own here. I do once more advise you join the OTO if you wish to get serious about things like this. It's a lot more fun when you're not alone ...

So far all the rituals that I've been talking about have been of the direct invocatory type, i.e., you invoke the energy from the gods directly into yourself. This is not the only method. An excellent form of ritual, especially when you're working with a group, is the Mass.

Basically the theory of a Mass is that you invoke a god or goddess into a priest or priestess, then that person transmits the power into another object (food or drink) which is consumed by the others present. By consuming the object (called the Host or Sacrament), all the people attending partake of the power of the gods. Since the divine power is in the Host, if the Host is in your body, the power is within you. From this simple theory you can develop very complex rituals. The Gnostic Mass which is practiced by many Thelemites all over the world on a regular basis is a good example of a fairly complicated Mass ritual.

The following is an example of a very simple Mass: the Mass of Baphomet. It is a group ritual, though if you're working totally alone, you should be able to adapt it for solo working. It was designed to be performed by beginning groups, so it is not difficult to organize. As well as that, there is no running around, so you can perform it in any size of room without too much problem. Be careful if you have thin walls though, because the chanting during the rite can get very loud, especially if you have more than half a dozen people.

First you will need a suitable food for the Sacrament. Red wine is always a good basic choice of drink for a Mass, so if in doubt you can use that. One group who practiced this rite used sugar cubes, since the cube is a symbol of Baphomet. This had the added advantage that sugar is a crystalline substance, and crystals have the ability to hold a charge of magical energy very well. Sugar cubes have the disadvantage that they are a bit hard to bite into though. The best solid food is

Cakes of Light, whose recipe you will find in the back of the book. If you are using cakes or cubes, you should have one for each person participating and no more. If you are using wine, drink all the wine during or immediately after the ritual. The charged or consecrated Host is a holy thing and must not be used for any other purpose except the magical one. All the people who will attend the Mass should be made aware beforehand that they must consume the consecrated Host. It is very bad practice to let someone watch without participating fully, as the magical energy can easily become unbalanced that way.

Before you start, the group should select two officers: one to be Manifester, one to be Banisher. If you wish, you can do this at random—throw dice, they are cubes too. Make a circle on the floor, big enough for all to sit in a ring inside it. Eight candles should be placed outside the circle. If your incense will be outside the circle, light it before you start and make sure that there is plenty of incense on the charcoal. If it will be inside the circle, make sure that someone is given the responsibility of looking after it so it doesn't get knocked over. You should also have a small bowl of salt water in the circle.

You should decide on some garb appropriate to Baphomet. If you have a copy of the famous picture of Baphomet drawn by Eliphas Levi, you might get some ideas. A necklace or bracelet that has been magically charged or is otherwise appropriate to Baphomet is very useful. A magical symbol on a card is also a good idea—an obvious one is Atu XV The Devil from the tarot pack. I've often used a large card painting of the eye in the triangle symbol.

Ensure that everyone has seen and studied the image of Baphomet as shown in the Tarot Atu or as in the Levi picture. Each person should attempt to memorize the picture as well as possible.

All sit within the circle in asana, facing the center. The Banisher may sit in the center (facing East) to begin with if you're short on space. The Manifester should sit in the

Western quarter. Begin by having the Banisher rise and perform a pentagram ritual. All the others should sit quietly in
meditation while this is going on, visualizing the symbols in
the quarters as the Banisher invokes them. Try to help the
Banisher astrally as the pentagrams are formed. When the
pentagram ritual is finished, the Banisher switches places with
the Manifester so that the Banisher is in the West and the
Manifester is in the center, facing East. The Manifester
should now put on whatever special garb you have prepared
and assume the characteristic position of the god. In the case
of Baphomet this is sitting cross-legged with the right hand
raised and the left hand lowered, with the first two fingers of
each hand outstretched and the last two fingers of each hand
curled into the palms. If you have a tarot card or other symbol prepared, it can be held in the lap of the Manifester. The
Sacrament should be placed just in front of the Manifester. If
you like, you can have someone read a poem or text here that
is appropriate to set the scene. The Thelemic Holy Book
Liber A'ash is an excellent choice.

Now comes the invocation proper. The celebrants
should begin to chant a mantra together. A simple one is
probably best—IAO is a good choice. They should attempt to
build up a good rhythm together, nice and slow to begin with,
picking up pace as the rite progresses. While they chant
everyone should visualize themselves as sitting on a blasted
heath, a cold dark landscape empty but for a solitary oak tree
and with lightning flashing around them. When this image
has been built up sufficiently, they should then visualize the
body of the Manifester in the form of Baphomet—an active
variation of the Assumption of God-forms technique. The
Manifester will slowly begin to feel the energy rise within as
the mantra and visualization grow stronger. It may help if the
Manifester chants the mantra too, but this is optional. Do
whatever feels best. It might be that for quite a while nothing
seems to happen, but keep going. Eventually you'll get to a
point when the power of Baphomet will really fill the body of
the Manifester. When possession is complete, the Manifester

falls forward, screaming the word LAShTAL, and places both hands on the Host, allowing the accumulated magick of Baphomet to flow into it. The celebrants stop the mantra dead at this moment.

The Manifester will usually be sitting trembling after this. Wait in silence for a few moments until everyone has calmed down a little. Then the Banisher should rise to stand in front of the Manifester and ensure that the force of possession has gone. If the Manifester is not fully back to normal consciousness, the Banisher should pick up the bowl of salt water and splash some over the Manifester's face, while calling the magical name of that person. When it is clear that everyone is fully back to Earth, the Host should be passed around the circle so that all the celebrants may consume it. All the celebrants must partake of the Host, and the Host should be fully consumed before the ritual goes on to the next part.

When all have consumed the Sacrament, the Manifester returns to the Western quarter, leaving the Banisher alone in the center of the circle to perform another pentagram ritual. Although you may be tempted to rush this one, do not yield to the temptation. The final banishing should be every bit as thorough as the first one, in order to preserve the symmetry of the rite and to fully clear the air in the temple.

Although this is a fairly simple ritual to plan and execute, you should find that it has a very strong effect. If you are part of a magical group that meets regularly, it's a good idea to perform this Mass at least once a month, changing officers each time so that each person gets a chance to play each part. One suggestion is that the Banisher from the first rite should be the Manifester in the second and a new Banisher chosen; the Banisher from the second rite becomes the Manifester in the third, etc. This way each new Manifester will learn how to do the banishings and get the feel of the rite, without being thrown in the deep end. Don't fall into the trap of allowing one or two people to dominate all the time, even though someone will say that they don't want to do it because they feel scared or embarrassed or whatever. Make sure that everyone participates fully.

Another good thing about this rite is that it is very easily customizable. When you have performed it a few times and feel confident with it, you can adapt it to invoke a different god or goddess. Find out all you can about the divinity that you wish to invoke—what it looks like, what would be an appropriate mantra, an appropriate text to be read, etc. Then just slot these things into the right places in the rite. Hey presto, you've got a general-purpose group ritual that you can work with for months or even years without getting bored.

***

When people ask me why I'm so into Crowley's work, I often explain it by comparing AC's relationship to magick with Einstein's relationship to physics. Each man turned an entire set of beliefs upside down by the application of a simple universal formula. In Einstein's case this formula was $E = mc^2$; in Crowley's case it was Thelema. But in each case there are many other formulae that have more specialized applications than these universal ones, since all systems and parts of systems operate largely by the application of formulae of one sort or another.

An important formula that you've already met is IAO, which I mentioned as a mantra for the Mass of Baphomet. The three letters of this formula stand for: Isis, Apophis, Osiris. These again are Egyptian deities, and I think most people reading this will have heard of them. Isis is a mother goddess, very similar to Nuit in many ways, but not quite so universal in scope—more close to the Earth. She is often portrayed as a woman enfolding the worshipper within her wings. In the formula she represents birth and new beginnings. Apophis is the destroyer god, who is often portrayed as a dragon or serpent. He represents the force that breaks down stability and destroys the old to make way for the new.

Osiris is the god of resurrection. He is portrayed with green skin, symbolizing the fertility of the crops that rise from the darkness of the ground. In his arms he carries a shepherd's crook and a farmer's flail, to emphasize the human working with nature. He represents life reborn.

This IAO formula thus encapsulates the essential process of all existence: birth, death, rebirth. It can be used to help you understand almost any process. For example take when you are trying to learn a new skill—a sport or even perhaps magick from this book(!). At first you try it, it's fun, you get a really good result—"beginner's luck." This is the Isis phase of the process. But then you decide to get more serious about things. You begin to practice, and soon what was once enjoyable and easy becomes boring and hard. You miss simple things and feel angry with yourself. You're in the Apophis phase. Nevertheless this phase is essential, for eventually you push past it, and the skills you've learned become automatic. Now you can start to really recapture the essence of the thing that attracted you in the first place in the Isis phase, coupled with the new technical abilities you've acquired in the Apophis phase. Together they form something new and even better: the Osiris phase.

This is only one explanation of the IAO formula; there are many others. I highly recommend that you sit down and really meditate on these three simple letters—you'll find them very useful indeed in your work.

An associated formula to IAO is one that I also mentioned in the Mass of Baphomet: LAShTAL. This strange-looking word is again tripartite. It is formed of LA, meaning Nothing in Hebrew; ShT, a variation of the name of the god Set, also an Egyptian destroyer god; and AL, meaning God in Hebrew. I think you should be able to see how this relates to IAO. But it is *not* the same thing! Each has a slightly different aspect. Rather than explain it in any detail, this time I'm going to leave this up to you to figure it out for yourself in your work.

* * *

In opposition to group workings like the Mass given above, there is one very important magical technique that is always a solitary one. This is the Invocation of the Holy Guardian Angel. The Holy Guardian Angel (or HGA as it is usually abbreviated) is an angel that is unique to each person—a special spiritual entity that guides and guards you. Now as to the reality of this or any other angel, the same theories apply as to the gods—whether or not they really exist, the universe *behaves* as though they exist. Or to put it another way: just because it's in your head doesn't make it less real—since everything is in your head all the time anyway. In fact Crowley states that one of the most important things about the Holy Guardian Angel is that it is such a ludicrous concept that no aspirant could ever possibly take it as being literally true.

There are many occult books that deal with the HGA as some form of Higher Self. This is nonsense, as anybody with even the slightest training in logic and grammar can see. By definition you can't have more than one self, otherwise it wouldn't be yourself, would it? And the idea of "Higher" being somehow better is stupid. Tall people aren't any better than short ones in my experience. The other problem with this Higher Self theory is that it implies that *you* are a Lower Self, somehow less worthy, which is a very dangerous belief to hold. To the Thelemite every man and every woman is a star, as you no doubt know by now.

Mathematically, if we call the universe "∞" (infinity) and I call myself "ME," we can describe the Holy Guardian Angel as: $HGA = \infty - ME$.

That is, my HGA is everything in the universe that I am not. So by linking up with my Holy Guardian Angel, I have access to the whole universe, both within myself and without myself. (Of course, one of the interesting things about this equation is that mathematically infinity minus anything is still infinity.) It's worth meditating on this simple equation; there is a lot more to it than meets the eye.

The Holy Guardian Angel is not a Higher Self; it is a completely individual being with its own personality and Will. It just so happens that its Will is to look after your development. This means that if you can communicate with your HGA, your magick will be hugely empowered, for the HGA can advise you how to direct your energies for the most effective results. The problem is that I cannot tell you how to do this. Since you are unique and your HGA is also unique, the relationship between you is unique. How I communicate with my HGA is not necessarily how you will communicate with yours. There are some points to consider, however. First, the relationship is one of Love, since it is the force of love that unites two things that are separate. In this loving relationship, the Aspirant usually plays the female role (regardless of what gender your body is now, to your HGA you are female), and the HGA plays the masculine role. This can be hard for heterosexual male magicians to cope with; I assume that it's easier for female heterosexuals and passive male homosexuals, but I have not yet enough data to fully judge. Comments from readers are welcomed on this issue.

Attaining communication with one's HGA (usually referred to as the Knowledge and Conversation of the Holy Guardian Angel) is not easy. Often it can take years of work. The traditional method of invocation involves locking yourself away for six months of concentrated prayer, not easy when you've got rent to pay. I personally did not use this method, not having a private income to rely on. To get in touch with my HGA, I used a short invocation taken from Liber LXV, a Thelemic Holy Book dealing with the relationship between the Aspirant and the Holy Guardian Angel. I highly recommend that if you are interested in contacting your HGA, you make this book your constant study and companion. You might also like to try using the word Adonai as a mantra. Adonai means "The Lord" and is the mystical title of your HGA. You must make your longing for Adonai your total reason for being. Every spare moment yearn for

Him. If you have ever felt overwhelming unrequited love for someone who ignores you (and who hasn't?), you'll know the kind of thing I mean.

If you wish, you can design a ritual that you think appropriate to call Him and perform it daily, but you can never know when and where He will make His presence felt. One friend of mine was stunned to find out that his HGA will only appear whenever he goes running. It really annoys him that he has to run five miles every time he needs a little advice, but that's magick for you. Whatever way you decide to work, remember that we're talking about something that will probably take a very long time—perhaps a lifetime's work, so don't be discouraged after a month. You haven't even scratched the surface in a month. Even if you get no obvious result, keep up your aspiration to the love of Adonai as often as you can. He will always be there anyway, trying to help you. The failure to communicate is not His fault but yours. You are like a radio receiver, He the broadcasting station. You have to learn how to tune in to what He is sending to you, and tune out all extraneous signals. Once you've done that you don't need me and this book anymore.

FURTHER STUDY

Magick—Appendix VI: The Gnostic Mass
Magick—Appendix VI: The Mass of the Phoenix
Magick—Appendix VII: Liber A'ash

Some Variations
on the Pentagram Ritual

There are dozens (maybe hundreds) of different variations on the pentagram ritual. The one I have given in the main body of the book is designed to be the most basic version so that you can learn the underlying structure of the rite. Once you understand this structure fully, you can try other versions or even design your own. If you do design your own, try to follow the "skeleton" I have shown you closely—this will ensure that you don't mess up too badly, I hope.

The first variation here is a rite used by the Golden Dawn magical Order. The G.D. is very well known in magical circles, and it was in this Order that Crowley did his earliest work. Over the past century the G.D. Lesser Pentagram Ritual has become the standard form, though personally I feel that it is somewhat outdated. I've never been a fan of this rite, and I don't really recommend it. But try it for yourself anyway; perhaps you'll disagree with me (many people do!). Note that in this rite you move deosil to banish, not widdershins. No, it doesn't make sense to me either.

The Lesser Banishing Ritual of the Pentagram

A. Qabalistic Cross.

Facing East, say

I. **Ateh,** (Unto Thee), forehead

II. **Malkuth,** (The Kingdom), breast

III. **ve-Geburah,** (and the Power), right

IV. **ve-Gedulah,** (and the Glory), left

V. **le-Olahm, Amen** (Forever, so be it), breast

B. Pentagram

EAST

VI. Trace banishing pentagram of Earth, (**Y H V H**)

SOUTH

VII. Trace banishing pentagram of Earth, (**A D N I**)

WEST

VIII. Trace banishing pentagram of Earth, (**A H I H**)

NORTH

IX. Trace banishing pentagram of Earth, (**A G L A**)

EAST

X. Form a cross and say:

XI. **Before me RAPHAEL.**

XII. **Behind me GABRIEL.**

XIII. **At my Right Hand MICHAEL.**

XIV. **At my Left Hand AURIEL.**

XV. **For about me flames the pentagram, and in the column stands the six-rayed star.**

C. Repeat Qabalistic cross.

***

The next variation is another one of my own rituals. This was one of the first attempts I made at designing a magical rite, and I still have a great affection for it. I was brought up doing the G.D. Pentagram as given above and became increasingly dissatisfied with it. For one thing, at the time I was not a big fan of Hebrew, and for another I found the Archangels that are invoked somewhat too masculine for my liking. So I decided to write a ritual that used ancient Egyptian instead of Hebrew, and goddesses instead of Archangels. The Rite of the Infinite Stars was the result. Women especially seem to like this one.

THE RITE OF THE INFINITE STARS

Face East and, assuming the god-form of Hoor-paar-kraat, draw your breath in deeply. Now expel the breath sharply, dashing your hand downward, with the words:

Tua Ra! (Hail Ra!)

The Cross of Light

Touching the forehead, say:

Tua-tu heru! (*The beings of heights worship thee!*)

Touching the genitals:

Tua-tu kheru! (*The beings of depths worship thee!*)

Touching the right shoulder:

Neb sésep. (*Lord of radiance.*)

Touching the left shoulder:

Khenti Het Hen. (*At the head of the Great House.*)

Crossing arms across the breast:

Hati-a en Kheperu! (*My heart, my coming into being!*)

The Pentagrams

Make a banishing pentagram of Earth in each quarter, charging it with the following words:

EAST: **Tuamautef.**

NORTH: **Hapi.**

WEST: **Qebsennuf.**

SOUTH: **Amset.**

Facing East again raise your arms to form a cross. Say:

Before me Neith.

Behind me Serq.

On my right hand Isis.

On my left hand Nephthys.

About me burn the stars of Nuit.

And within me burns the star of Hadit.

Tua Ra!

Repeat the Cross of Light as before, finishing in the sign of Hoor-paar-kraat.

***

LIBER V VEL REGULI

A∴A∴ publication in Class D.
Being the Ritual of the Mark of the Beast:
an incantation proper to invoke the
Energies of the Aeon of Horus,
adapted for the daily use of the
Magician of whatever grade.

With commentaries by Frater Hermes Eimi OTO 1994 e.v.
(Identified by italics and full-width text.)

[The title is Latin and means Book 5 or Book of the Prince. Regulus is also the name of the star which marks the beginning or 0 degree of the constellation Leo.]

THE FIRST GESTURE.

The Oath of the Enchantment which is called The Elevenfold Seal.

THE ANIMADVERSION TOWARD THE AEON.

1. Let the Magician, robed and armed as he may deem to be fit, turn his face toward Boleskine, that is the House of The Beast 666. {Note 1: Boleskine House is on Loch Ness, 17 miles from Inverness, Latitude 57.14 N. Longitude 4.28 W.}

[Note that this implies that the direction of Boleskine should be taken as "East" in the temple, as is specified in Liber XV, the Gnostic Mass. However it does not necessarily have to be so. Since later the text specifies that the Magician must grasp his Wand, the "robed and armed as he may deem to be fit" is not as wide-ranging as it may sound.]

2. Let him strike the battery 1-3-3-3-1.

[*Eleven knocks, eleven being the number of magical energy—
see Liber AL I, 60. Note that there are four sets of eleven
knocks during the complete ritual, making 44 in total, representing the materialization of magical energy, and also being
a number of Ra-Hoor-Khuit. See Liber XLIV, The Mass of
the Phoenix.*]

3. Let him put the Thumb of his right hand between
its index and medius, and make the gestures here-
after following.

[*The thumb being the finger attributed to Spirit, and also containing an important center of cakkric energy. Again see also
Liber XV.*]

THE VERTICAL COMPONENT OF THE ENCHANTMENT.

1. Let him describe a circle about his head, crying,
NUIT!

[*The Sahashara Cakkra, above the head, attributed to Ain
Soph on the Tree of Life.*]

2. Let him draw the Thumb vertically downward
and touch the Muladhara Cakkra, crying, **HADIT!**

[*The Muladhara (Earth center, attributed to Malkuth on the
Tree of Life) is found at the base of the spine, or at the per-
ineum just behind the genital region (opinions differ). I'd suggest the latter in practice, since touching the base of the spine
during the rite is somewhat awkward.*]

3. Let him, retracing the line, touch the center of his breast and cry **RA-HOOR-KHUIT!**

[The Anahata Cakkra—the solar center, attributed to Tiphareth, or perhaps more accurately to the triangle Chesed, Geburah, Tiphareth. This will especially make sense to initiates of the Second Degree of OTO. Note that the symbol of Ra-Hoor-Khuit is a downward-pointing red triangle of fire.]

THE HORIZONTAL COMPONENTS OF THE ENCHANTMENT.

1. Let him touch the Center of his Forehead, his mouth, and his larynx, crying, **AIWAZ!**

[The center of the forehead is the location of the Ajna Cakkra, the larynx the location of the Vishuddha Cakkra, attributed to Saturn and Da'ath. The mouth is the only one of these which is not a primary Cakkra—perhaps because Aiwaz is the voice of the gods—see Liber AL. Interestingly the mouth is a minor Cakkra—the Kala Cakkra.]

2. Let him draw his thumb from right to left across his face at the level of the nostrils.

[This forms the cross-path on the Tree of Life from Binah to Chokmah—the path of The Empress.]

3. Let him touch the center of his breast and his solar plexus, crying, **THERION!**

[The Anahata again and the Manipura. Both of these together are attributed to the Chesed, Geburah, Tiphareth triangle; I know this is odd, but that's just one of the problems of trying to relate two widely varying systems. The Tree of Life has only five Sephiroth on the Middle Pillar, whereas the yoga system used here has seven primary Cakkras.]

4. Let him draw his thumb from left to right across his breast at the level of the sternum.

[*The cross-path linking Chesed to Geburah, the path of Lust.*]

5. Let him touch the Svadisthana, and the Muladhara Cakkra, crying, **BABALON!**

[*The Svadisthana is located in the genital region, attributed to Yesod and the Moon.*]

6. Let him draw his thumb from right to left across his abdomen, at the level of the hips. (Thus shall he formulate the Sigil of the Grand Hierophant, but dependent from the Circle.)

[*The cross-path linking Hod and Netzach on the Tree, the path of The Tower. Note that the numerological value of the three cross-paths added together is 93. I don't know why the crossbars go in these directions. They don't follow the path of the Lightning Flash as it shoots downward from Kether to Malkuth—perhaps there may be a reference to the direction of spin of the cakkras. The Sigil of the Grand Hierophant is the triple cross.*]

THE ASSEVERATION OF THE SPELLS.

1. Let the Magician clasp his hands upon his Wand, his fingers and thumbs interlaced, crying, **LA-ShTAL! THELEMA! FIAOF! AGAPE! AUMGN!**
    (Thus shall be declared the Words of Power whereby the Energies of the Aeon of Horus work his will in the World.)

[*Each of these Words has the numerical value of 93. Since there are five of them and they are repeated once, plus an extra THELEMA in the middle, there are a total of 11 "93" Words in the rite. Note that the F's in FIAOF are silent, as is the GN in AUMGN. For more on these words see Book 4 Part III, Magick in Theory & Practice. Furthermore, in this First Gesture there are six god names mentioned: Nuit, Hadit, Ra-Hoor-Khuit, Aiwaz, Therion, Babalon; and five "93" words. Eleven invocations in total, thus is it named The Elevenfold Seal. The combination of the six and five is a very important facet of the rite—see section 23, lines h & i.]*

THE PROCLAMATION OF THE ACCOMPLISHMENT.

1. Let the Magician strike the Battery: 3-5-3, crying, **ABRAHADABRA.**

THE SECOND GESTURE.

THE ENCHANTMENT.

1. Let the Magician, still facing Boleskine, advance to the circumference of his circle.

2. Let him turn himself toward the left and pace with the stealth and swiftness of a tiger the precincts of his circle, until he complete one revolution thereof.

3. Let him give the Sign of Horus (or The Enterer) as he passeth, so to project the force that radiateth from Boleskine before him.

[This sign is made by leaning forward, advancing the left foot and throwing the arms out horizontally before you, pointing with the index fingers as if to fire energy out of them.]

4. Let him pace his path until he comes to the North; there let him halt and turn his face to the North.

[*That is you go round one and a quarter times.*]

5. Let him trace with his wand the Averse Pentagram proper to invoke Air (Aquarius).

[*An averse pentagram is one with the single point down, two points up. The Averse Air pentagram is drawn by starting at the bottom left point and going horizontally across to the right, then up left, down middle, up right, down left, i.e., go widdershins (counterclockwise). In other words it is like an upright Air Pentagram rotated through 180 degrees.*]

6. Let him bring the wand to the center of the Pentagram and call upon **NUIT!**

[*You should visualize the particular god or goddess called in each quarter. If in doubt use the tarot imagery. For Nuit, see Atu XVII, The Star; Atu XX, The Aeon; or Atu XXI, The Universe.*]

7. Let him make the sign called Puella, standing with his feet together, head bowed, his left hand shielding the Muladhara Cakkra, and his right hand shielding his breast (attitude of the Venus de Medici).

[*And where do you hold the wand while you're doing this? One solution is to grip it between your knees when you're making these signs. Yes, I know it doesn't sound too elegant, but it works.*]

8. Let him turn again to the left, and pursue his Path as before, projecting the force from Boleskine as he passeth; let him halt when he next cometh to the South and face outward.

[*i.e., go round one half circle.*]

9. Let him trace the Averse Pentagram that invoketh Fire (Leo).

[*Start bottom middle and go deosil (clockwise), i.e., go up left and then round until you've completed the entire pentagram.*]

10. Let him point his wand to the center of the Pentagram, and cry **HADIT!**

[*See Atu XX, The Aeon—Hadit is the winged disk.*]

11. Let him give the sign Puer, standing with feet together, and head erect. Let his right hand (the thumb extended at right angles to the fingers) be raised, the forearm vertical at a right angle with the upper arm, which is horizontally extended in the line joining the shoulders. Let his left hand, the thumb extended forward and the fingers clenched, rest at the junction of the thighs (attitude of the gods Mentu, Khem, etc.).

12. Let him proceed as before; then in the East, let him make the Averse Pentagram that invoketh Earth (Taurus).

[*This time go round a quarter circle. The pentagram is drawn from bottom middle widdershins toward the upper right point and so on.*]

13. Let him point his wand to the center of the pentagram, and cry, **THERION!**

[See Atu XI, Lust—Therion is the Beast pictured.]

14. Let him give the sign called Vir, the feet being together. The hands, with clenched finger and thumbs thrust out forward, are held to the temples; the head is then bowed and pushed out as if to symbolize the buffing of an horned beast (attitude of Pan, Bacchus, etc.). (Frontispiece, *Equinox I*, iii).

15. Proceeding as before, let him make in the West the Averse Pentagram whereby Water is invoked.

[The Averse Pentagram of Water: start at the bottom right and go across to the bottom left and thus round deosil. Note that the pentagrams change direction each time—first widdershins, then deosil, then widdershins again, then deosil.]

16. Pointing the wand to the center of the Pentagram, let him call upon **BABALON!**

[See Atu XI again—Babalon is the goddess riding on the Beast. Note that you "call upon" Nuit & Babalon but "cry" the other names. This may be significant in that the LA (feminine) forces are perceived as lying outside the direct sphere of your influence and are requested in a softer manner than the masculine forces.]

17. Let him give the sign Mulier. The feet are widely separated, and the arms raised so as to suggest a crescent. The head is thrown back (attitude of Baphomet, Isis in Welcome, the Microcosm of Vitruvius). (See *Book 4*, Part II).

[You can't grip your wand between your knees here, so hold it in your hand I guess ...]

18. Let him break into the dance, tracing a centripetal spiral widdershins, enriched by revolutions upon his axis as he passeth each quarter, until he come to the center of the circle. There let him halt, facing Boleskine.

[*You go round the circle one complete revolution here. You've now done three and a half circles, the number of coils of the Kundalini, amongst other things. Compare the Priestess's dance in Liber XV, the Gnostic Mass, and note that 15 = 3 x 5. Also note that you have gone from Earth through Air, Water, and Fire, and thus to Spirit in the center. You have raised yourself from the realm of the material to the world beyond.*]

19. Let him raise the wand, trace the Mark of the Beast and cry **AIWAZ!**

[*The Mark of the Beast is a sign in the form of a solar circle with a dot in the middle, and below it a lunar crescent with two small crescents below that. You can draw it in one motion by going round the circle once, then making a wider arc to draw the crescent, then going back in two loops under the crescent. Yes, I know this still sounds pretty vague, but it's the best I can think of right now. As the pentagrams are symbols of the four material elements, so is the Mark of the Beast the symbol of Spirit. Aiwaz should be visualized as "a tall dark man in his thirties, well-knit, active and strong, with the face of a savage king, and eyes veiled lest their gaze destroy what they saw."*]

20. Let him trace the invoking Hexagram of The Beast.

[*This is the Unicursal Hexagram, drawn from the top middle point deosil toward the bottom right, top left, bottom middle, top right, bottom left, top middle.*]

21. Let him lower the wand, striking the Earth therewith.

[*The conception here is that you are bringing the Thelemic current from above down to the Earth. You are standing in both worlds and can act as a bridge between them.*]

22. Let him give the sign of Mater Triumphans (The feet are together; the left arm is curved as if it supported a child; the thumb and index finger of the right hand pinch the nipple of the left breast, as if offering it to that child). Let him utter the word **THELEMA!**

[*The child being the Thelemic magical current that you have set in motion, that you have birthed upon the Earth.*]

23. Perform the spiral dance, moving deosil and whirling widdershins.

[*As you have moved widdershins before to banish, so now you move deosil to invoke.*]

Each time on passing the West extend the wand to the Quarter in question, and bow:

[*Note that you extend the wand to the quarter, not bow to the quarter. Each time you bow to the West I assume, since bowing upward, for example, is rather difficult.*]

    a. **Before me the powers of LA!** (to West.)
    b. **Behind me the powers of AL!** (to East.)
    c. **On my right hand the powers of LA!** (to North.)
    d. **On my left hand the powers of AL!"** (to South.)

    e. **Above me the powers of ShT!"** (leaping in the air.)

    f. **Beneath me the powers of ShT!'** (striking the ground.)

[*LA means Nothing and is directed to the West & North, since these are the negative, feminine quarters. AL means god and is directed to the positive, masculine quarters. Note that we do not assume that positive is "better" than negative— it is simply a different polarity, as in an electrical current. ShT is the child of negative and positive energies, and the force that reconciles them. LA = 31, AL = 31, ShT = 31; thus 3 x 31 = 93*]

    g. **Within me the Powers!** (in the attitude of Phthah erect, the feet together, the hands clasped upon the vertical wand.)

[*Phthah is the Creator God of Egypt. The conception is that you have built your own universe. I always find that this rite increases my creative powers greatly. For this reason it is to be particularly recommended to all those engaged in artistic pursuits.*

    Note that you've now done seven more circles, which is twice three and a half, so altogether in the rite you've gone round three and a half widdershins, then twice three and a half deosil, making a total of three times three and a half or only once, depending on whether you count the widdershins circumambulations as a positive or negative amount.]

    h. **About me flames my Father's face, the Star of Force and Fire.**

[*My Father is this case is Baphomet, the All-Father of the Knights Templar. The Averse Pentagram is occasionally drawn with Baphomet's face within its points, the two upward points being the horns, the lowest point his beard. See the well-known logo of the Church of Satan.]*

i. And in the Column stands His six-rayed Splendor!

[Note: flames, father's, face, force, fire. Five F's. Qabalistically, F is Vau = 6, thus we have the 5 and 6 combined. 5 x 6 = 30. Stands, six-rayed, splendor. Three S's. Qabalistically, S is Samekh = 60. 3 x 60 = 180. Plus the 30 from the previous line gives us a total of 210 = NOX.]

(This dance may be omitted, and the whole utterance chanted in the attitude of Phthah.)

THE FINAL GESTURE.

This is identical with the First Gesture.

Cakes of Light

Ingredients

$1/2$ gallon (2 liters) of port wine
$1\,1/2$ cups of whole-wheat flour
Honey (to taste)
$1\,1/2$ tablespoons of olive oil
Abra-melin oil (to taste—not much!)
Other ingredient (see AL III, 23 and 24)

Procedure

Heat the wine at the lowest heat possible. Steam should be rising, but it should never boil. Let it simmer for approximately five hours. At the end you should have about a quarter of an inch (half a centimeter) of goo at the bottom of the pot.

In a mixing bowl add the flour, honey, wine goo, olive oil, and Abra-melin oil. (You can get Abra-melin oil from an occult supply shop or ask your local OTO.) Knead until it becomes cookie dough—this takes a while. Add more flour if it's too sticky.

Take a very small amount of the dough, add a small (homeopathic) amount of the other ingredient to it, and make it into a single small cake. Turn the oven up to its highest setting and bake this single cake until it is burned black. Take it from the oven and crush it into powdery ash, then add the ashes to the original dough mixture.

Roll out the dough on a floured surface. Flour the rolling pin and your hands too. When the dough has been flattened out, cut into cakes using a small circular cutter—a pill bottle top or lipstick top is ideal.

Reduce the oven heat to 300°F (or approximately 150°C).

Place the cakes on a floured sheet and bake them in the oven for no more than five minutes. Usually three to four minutes is enough. The cakes won't look done when you take them out—just let them cool for a while, and they'll be fine, hardening as they cool.

EPILOGUE

That's the end of the book. It was short, I know, but I'd rather not kill trees just to add more waffle to make myself look important. Just about everything you really need to know has been covered here, I hope. If you disagree, let me know, and I'll put it in the next edition. I do know that there's enough here to keep even a good student going for at least a year.

Having said all that, I do realize that there are many things not covered here—evocation of spirits being one that immediately springs to mind, but one of my ideals in writing this book was to give only rituals and exercises that I had personally tried and that were reasonably original. Although I have evoked spirits on many occasions, I do not feel that I have anything original to offer in this field. Likewise for the other stuff I've left out.

In this book I did not want to simply regurgitate the work of Crowley, as so many authors both Thelemic and non-Thelemic are wont to do—often without giving AC even the slightest bit of credit for his pioneering efforts. I cheerfully and humbly acknowledge that everything here ultimately derives from Liber AL and other Thelemic works that have emerged from the pen of To Mega Therion. I also would like to assert my belief that it is our job to continue and build upon that work to create a fully realized Thelemic esoteric and exoteric culture. From that belief springs this book.

There are many other possibilities for further exploration now that you've grown up a little and no longer need me to hold your hand. Consult the suggested reading list that follows and get another perspective on everything. Doubt all that I've told you. Do *not* believe anything I say (especially this sentence). Remember that only experience truly counts for anything in this world, but don't forget that the experiences of others are just as valid as your own, even if they are completely different.

No book exists in isolation, and this one is no exception. I would like to take this opportunity to express my thanks to the many coworkers who have inspired and helped me over the years.

Firstly, the three wise Magi who guided my first footsteps on the path: Brother Bobby Menary, who saw me not for what I was, but for what I would become, and gave me the greatest gift that anyone could ever wish for; Brother R.B.B. for showing me that Wisdom is the child of experience, the true Crown; and Frater Marabas, for teaching me that the Great Work really is *work*, and just how much I was capable of achieving when I really tried.

Secondly, I would like to thank my Leeds University Occult Society contemporaries who helped me develop as a magician, especially the three unwise boys: Frater Muladorio for showing me a different perspective on Thelema, even though I rarely agreed with him; Frater Impecunius, who helped me experiment with much of what eventually ended up in this book; and Frater Abaddon, whose collaborations with me were always productive, educational, and above all, great fun.

Thirdly, I would like to thank the initiators who brought me to the Sanctuary: Frater Hyperion, whose knowledge and understanding (and endless patience) have been of incalculable assistance; Soror Laetitia, for being such a perfect avatar of Nuit; and Frater 218, for introducing me to a world I had waited many years to visit.

In addition the beta testers without whom this book would have been only half of what it is now: Ruth, Gina, Claus, and most especially Miriam, whose questions gave me the idea in the first place. Dustin for her encouragement and for the Cakes of Light recipe. Frater P.A.L. whose keen intellect has given me lots to think about. My beloved Sisters, Jessica, Ariana, and Kat for assisting in the genesis of this second edition. And most especially, my dear Sister LOA who has been a continuous font of wise counsel and assistance over the years, as well as a great Priestess.

But above all, I dedicate this book to all my Sisters and Brothers of Ordo Templi Orientis, whose friendship, support, and enthusiasm have been a source of endless joy to me in my travels round the world. I hope that by reading this book you have been able to share in some of that joy.

If you genuinely feel that Thelema is the way for you, join the OTO. Participate in the Gnostic Mass if your local OTO body is performing it. Help build the Thelemic culture that I speak of. The knowledge that I have given to you was given to me freely, with the understanding that it was my responsibility to pass it on to any others who might need it; now it is your turn to do likewise.

Love is the law, love under will.

RODNEY ORPHEUS

ORDO TEMPLI ORIENTIS
JAF Box 7666
New York, NY 10116
USA

SUGGESTED READING

In the following section I have tried to give a reasonably structured and comprehensive listing of books that the student may find valuable. Please be aware that generally speaking occult books (like most things in the world) follow Sturgeon's Law: "90 percent of everything is crud." So in choosing the books to recommend I have simply listed what I have read and found useful enough to keep in my own library—you may well disagree with my choices or get nothing from them, in which case look for other books that will give you what you need. In any case, it is advisable to read as widely as possible, and as critically as possible—never accept any written assertion about magick (or anything else for that matter) at face value. Experiment for yourself, prove or disprove the validity of the assertions. This goes for the book you are now reading as well, of course.

In the section called Magick you will find books that by and large have a Thelemic perspective, but that may not necessarily agree with the methods given in this book. Again I suggest that you try out whatever seems interesting to you, and make up your own mind as to what is the most useful way for you to work. If in doubt, I recommend that you stick to the methods that I have given, not just because I think that they are the best but because everything in this book links together into one unified system. Think of what I have given here as the main course, and the other books as items in the salad bar—take whatever you need to add extra flavor.

You don't have to read all the books I have listed, but I do recommend that you read at least one or two from each group. The division into groups is occasionally a little arbitrary but hopefully makes things a bit more convenient for the reader. One of the biggest problems facing every beginner is simply knowing where to start, and I hope this should help somewhat.

Note that Aleister Crowley manages to rear his head in just about every section listed. This alone should convince you that his books are well worth studying, since he manages to cover an immense variety of ground, and all his works link together, so each one you read helps you to understand the others better.

You will see that there is also a large Science and Philosophy section. I wholeheartedly agree with Crowley's advice that the serious student of magick should obtain a good all-round knowledge of these two subjects. All too often I have met well-read and practiced occultists who still had no real depth of understanding of magick, simply because they were incapable of logically examining the basic parameters of their own world, both inside and outside themselves. In this Science and Philosophy section I have listed both books which are "magically" oriented and books which are "hard science" oriented, without attempting to differentiate between them. This is intentional, as to my mind the difference is largely illusory. "We place no reliance on virgin or pigeon—our method is science, our aim is religion."

As well as the books I have listed in the S and P group, it will be useful for the student to gain some basic knowledge in the sciences generally and also a good grounding in traditional philosophy, especially European mathematical logic and Buddhist religious philosophy (I use the term "religious" rather loosely here).

Another tip: books are expensive, so if you are short of cash, remember that libraries lend you books for free (you'd be amazed at the number of people who never bother to think of this). If your local library is run by conservative forces who would rather not stock such dangerous and mind-expanding works as the ones I have listed here, just request that they obtain them for you, which should be a fairly simple and painless procedure. As a teenager growing up in a country village in Ireland, I had absolutely no way of getting hold of occult books. My village didn't have a bookshop at all, so the fact that I had no money was irrelevant. However, the village did have a small library with *one* occult book, which had a reading list like this one at the back. Six months and several dozen request cards later that little library had the best collection of magical textbooks in the country, and only one person who wanted to read them. Hey presto! Instant personal (free) occult library—and a beautiful young librarian to replace the old one who had to retire because of overwork.

Anyway, enough reminiscing.

THELEMA

Aleister Crowley
  The Holy Books of Thelema
  The Law is for All
  Liber Aleph
  Magick Without Tears
John W. Parsons: *Freedom is a Two-Edged Sword*

MAGICK

Michael Bertiaux: *The Voudon Gnostic Workbook*
David Conway: *Magic: An Occult Primer*
Aleister Crowley: *Magick: Book 4*
Louis T. Culling: *The Complete Magick Curriculum of the G.B.G.*
Lon DuQuette
  Aleister Crowley's Illustrated Goetia
  Enochian World of Aleister Crowley
  The Magick of Thelema
Anton LaVey
  The Satanic Bible
  The Satanic Rituals
Israel Regardie: *The Tree of Life*
Ray Sherwin
  The Book of Results
  The Theatre of Magick
James Wasserman: *The Magical Diary*

Tarot and Qabalah

Frater Achad
  The Anatomy of the Body of God
  Q.B.L.
Aleister Crowley: *The Book of Thoth*
Lon DuQuette
  Aleister Crowley's Thoth Tarot
  The Chicken Qabalah
Dion Fortune: *The Mystical Qabalah*
Israel Regardie: *A Garden of Pomegranates*

Yoga

Aleister Crowley
  Book Four, Part I
  Eight Lectures on Yoga
Nik Douglas and Penny Slinger: *Sexual Secrets*

History of Magick

Kenneth Grant: *The Magical Revival*
Ellic Howe: *The Magicians of the Golden Dawn*
King and Sutherland: *The Rebirth of Magic*
Martin P. Starr: *The Unknown God*
Colin Wilson: *The Occult*

Life of Crowley

Aleister Crowley: *The Confessions of Aleister Crowley*
Richard Kaczynski: *Perdurabo: The Life of Aleister Crowley*
Israel Regardie: *The Eye in the Triangle*
John Symonds: *The King of the Shadow Realm*

SCIENCE AND PHILOSOPHY

Angerford and Lea: *Thundersqueak*
Fritjof Capra: *The Tao of Physics*
Mabel Collins: *Light on the Path*
Aleister Crowley
  The Book of Lies
  Little Essays Toward Truth
Stephen Hawking: *A Brief History of Time*
Nick Herbert: *Quantum Reality*
Benjamin Hoff: *The Tao of Pooh*
Julian Jaynes: *The Origin of Consciousness in the Breakdown*
  of the Bicameral Mind
Lao Zi: *Dao De Jing*
Desmond Morris
  Manwatching
  The Naked Ape
Carl Sagan: *Dragons of Eden*
Alvin Toffler
  Future Shock
  The Third Wave
Robert Anton Wilson
  Cosmic Trigger
  The Illuminati Papers
  The New Inquisition
  Quantum Psychology

FICTION

James Branch Cabell: *Jurgen*
Aleister Crowley
  Diary of a Drug Fiend
  Konx Om Pax
  Moonchild
John Crowley: *Little, Big*

Dion Fortune
   The Demon Lover
   The Goat-Foot God
   Moon Magic
   The Sea Priestess
   The Winged Bull
Robert Shea: *All Things Are Lights*
Robert Anton Wilson
   Chronicles
   The Historical Illuminatus
   Masks of the Illuminati

Also highly recommended for meditation: the Alice books by Lewis Carroll and the Winnie-the-Pooh books by A. A. Milne

ROLE-PLAYING GAMES

Call of Cthulu (Sandy Petersen)
Hidden Tradition (Rodney Orpheus)
Illuminati (Steve Jackson)
Neverwinter Nights (BioWare)

About the Author

Rodney Orpheus has been a practicing occultist since the age of fourteen, a member of the Ordo Templi Orientis for over fifteen years, and currently serves as the Grand Treasurer General of the UK Grand Lodge. An established musician, he belongs to a band called The Cassandra Complex, one of the most important electro-industrial bands of the past decade. He remains active in the music industry, performing with, recording, producing, and advising some of today's top acts. Rodney lives in London and travels extensively. This is his first book.

To Our Readers

Weiser Books, an imprint of Red Wheel/Weiser, publishes books across the entire spectrum of occult and esoteric subjects. Our mission is to publish quality books that will make a difference in people's lives without advocating any one particular path or field of study. We value the integrity, originality, and depth of knowledge of our authors.

Our readers are our most important resource, and we appreciate your input, suggestions, and ideas about what you would like to see published. Please feel free to contact us, to request our latest book catalog, or to be added to our mailing list.

Red Wheel/Weiser, LLC
665 Third Street, Suite 400
San Francisco, CA 94107
www.redwheelweiser.com